WISDOM *for* HOME PRESERVERS

WISDOM *for* HOME PRESERVERS

500 TIPS FOR PICKLING, CANNING, CURING, SMOKING, AND MORE

ROBIN RIPLEY

The Taunton Press

The Taunton Press
Inspiration for hands-on living®

The Taunton Press, Inc., 63 South Main Street
P.O. Box 5506, Newtown, CT 06470-5506
e-mail: tp@taunton.com

Conceived, designed, and produced by
Quid Publishing
Level 4 Sheridan House
114 Western Road
Hove BN3 1DD
www.quidpublishing.com

Library of Congress Cataloging-in-Publication Data

Ripley, Robin, author.
  Wisdom for home preservers : 500 tips for pickling, canning, curing,
smoking & more / Robin Ripley.
     pages cm
    Summary: "This book features 500 tips and techniques; ten chapters
(one for each method) provide detailed, practical information, including
storing and troubleshooting, while basic recipes help novice home
preservers get started"-- Provided by publisher.
  ISBN 978-1-62710-711-2 (hardback)
1. Canning and preserving. 2. Curing. 3. Food--Preservation. I.
Title.
  TX601.R57 2014
  641.4'2--dc23
                            2014014653

Printed in China

10 9 8 7 6 5 4 3 2 1

For Harry—my husband
and best friend

CONTENTS

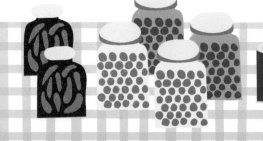

INTRODUCTION

Our grandmothers (and perhaps a few grandfathers) preserved food as insurance—a way to guarantee there would be food during the dark, cold winter days. Today, we can have dinner delivered in 30 minutes by ordering from our cell phones. Food preserving is less about making sure we won't go hungry and more about meeting other important needs. For some home preservers, it's another way to stretch the grocery budget. For others, it's a way to explore their culinary creativity. And for others, it's a way to manage food sensitivities and allergies. These 500 practical, down-to-earth tips will guide readers through the food preserving basics to create a shelf-full—or a whole pantry and freezer-full—of safe and delicious foods the whole family will appreciate.

GETTING
STARTED

With all the full-color cookbooks and chef-inspired television shows, it's tempting to plunge right in to your first preserving project with little more than enthusiasm, a recipe, and hope. But there are basic building blocks that must be observed to ensure that those hopes aren't dashed. To make the preserving process as enjoyable, simple, and foolproof as possible, learn the planning and organizing tips that master preservers know.

BEFORE YOU BEGIN

TIP 1: *Focus your efforts by reflecting on your motivations and goals*

● Everyone has his or her own motivations for canning, drying, freezing, or tackling some other food preserving project. Having a ready supply of healthy food, reducing your carbon footprint, saving money, preserving your homegrown fruits and vegetables, improved taste and quality, and connecting with the past are all excellent reasons for tackling a home food preservation project. Besides, most people find it satisfying and even fun!

If you take a few minutes to consider your motivations for a new preserving project, you'll have a more focused direction for your efforts. For example, if preserving your garden harvest is what's inspiring you, you'll want to time your preserving projects with expected harvest dates and begin researching recipes for the types of fruits and vegetables you grow. If saving money is the motivator, research the most economical farmers' markets, produce stands, or pick-your-own farms. If you're enthusiastic about exploring your family's culinary history and traditions, you may want to visit with your older relatives and ask for family recipes before they are lost to time. These ideas will help shape your direction and focus how to spend your time.

TIP 2: *Appreciate the nutritional value of home-preserved foods*

⬤ Your primary motivation for canning, freezing, drying, and fermenting may not be improved nutrition. But as you experiment and begin to compare your homemade products with their store-bought equivalents, you'll soon appreciate what a nutrition boost you're giving yourself and your family. Processed and packaged foods are filled with stabilizers, artificial colors, excess sodium, unnecessary sugar, and other multisyllabic ingredients most of us can't pronounce. When you preserve your own food—and especially if you grow what you preserve yourself—you control exactly what's going into the jar, bag, or freezer. And besides, having a ready supply of food will make expensive and calorie-laden restaurant meals much less tempting.

TIP 3: *Understand why foods spoil*

🌀 Everything associated with life has an expiration date. Foods are no exception, and food deterioration and eventual spoilage is a perfectly natural process. It's not just one factor that functions to spoil food, but a whole host of factors. Understanding them will help you appreciate the safety guidelines that go along with all food preserving projects.

The most obvious damage to foods comes from physical damage and pantry pests, such as bugs, worms, mice, and other critters, so it's obvious that you must take care in handling food and to exclude critters from places where you will store it. Somewhat less obvious, but still observable, factors working to destroy food are light and temperature. Light can change the color of food and destroy vitamins. Temperatures that are too high or too low cause observable physical changes such as drying out or freezing. But warm temperatures also make foods vulnerable to attack by microorganisms, such as bacteria, yeasts, and molds. And then there are enzymes. Enzymes are naturally present in all food. It is enzymes at work that cause changes in texture, flavor, and color, as when a banana turns brown and becomes mushy. Food preserving usually involves steps to stop or delay enzyme action in foods. The final factor is time, the ultimate destroyer. Nothing lasts forever, not even carefully preserved food.

TIP 4: *Utilize social networking and online classified ads to find no- or low-cost preserving equipment and supplies*

● Before launching into your first preserving project, assemble a list of the equipment and supplies you'll need. (We have provided suggested equipment lists on pages 283–284.) You can head to the store and purchase everything new. Or you can go on a bit of a scavenger hunt and find used or barely used equipment for little or no money at all.

Start by asking friends and family if they have canning or other equipment and supplies they no longer need or want. Many people are happy to let you clear their basements of canning jars, crocks, canners, and other useful goodies they no longer use. Scan for freebies and post notices on classified ad websites. If you enjoy yard sales and thrift stores, make a habit of scanning through the kitchen items for equipment that you don't have. Remember to keep an eye out for useful bowls, containers, and trays so that you have a variety to choose from.

If you need free or low-cost produce, make a deal with a gardener friend to swap your finished canned goods for their produce. If you plan far enough in advance, you can even start your own backyard garden to grow the produce you'll need. With some ingenuity and a little time, you won't need a lot of money to get started.

TIP 5: *Save the dates*

Most home preservers' busiest times coincide with the harvest, when fruits and vegetables come rolling in by the bushel full from the garden or pick-your-own farm. Harvest season is also when fresh produce at farmers' markets is piled high. If you envision large-scale preserving projects, save up vacation days from work or block out a couple of Saturdays when produce is likely to be at its freshest and most bountiful. You'll want the extra time set aside to deal with the cleaning, processing, labeling, and storing.

Your local agricultural extension office should have a calendar of when different fruits and vegetables are ripe in your area. Alternatively, consult the seasonal produce guideline on page 19. If stocking a pantry shelf full of tomato sauces is on your To Do list, block out time in late summer when the deluge of tomatoes is at its peak. If shelves of strawberry preserves are your heart's desire, then early spring is the time to save the date. You'll be glad you planned your project in advance.

TIP 6: *Recruit help*

Small-batch preserving projects can be rewarding to accomplish all by yourself. But if you're going to undertake a day-long or two-day marathon canning session, recruit help, particularly for time-consuming activities such as washing, peeling, pitting, and chopping. Many hands make light work and will make the whole project less exhausting. Try to make the work as fun and enjoyable as possible for your recruits. Play music, offer lunch, and schedule breaks. Bribes are usually an effective means of securing cooperation from friends and teenagers—actually, almost anyone!

TIP 7: *Find a community canning kitchen*

⚫ Some civic organizations, local governments, and church groups, particularly in rural and farming areas, sponsor community canning days to pool resources, labor, and equipment for canning projects. These kitchens are often located in churches, schools, or community centers and many offer classes and instruction as well. Some community canning kitchens are staffed with knowledgeable managers and equipped with commercial-grade equipment that make short work of large-scale projects. Consult your local agricultural extension service or master preserver program to find a location and date near you.

TIP 8: *Take a food preserving class*

⚫ People learn in different ways. If you prefer an instructional or hands-on class over a self-study approach to learning food preserving, then look into classes that might be offered by your local agricultural extension service, parks and recreation department, or even your local library. If none are available, you may be able to find enough like-minded people interested in attending a class to convince one of those groups to organize a program.

In addition, there are thousands of free online videos for various food preserving techniques. You may find some DVDs available for checkout from your local library. Some universities also offer free online classes for food preserving that are available to anyone with computer access.

SOURCING AND PREPARING PRODUCE

TIP 9: *Preserve what you have and what you love*

● If you are new to preserving, it may be a little bewildering to know where to begin. Should you learn canning first? Or fill the freezer? Should you learn to make pickles? Or would it be better to dry treats for after-school snacks?

When taking your first steps in preserving, it's a good idea to begin with what you have and what you love. If you have an overabundance of cucumbers from your backyard garden, you can start with putting up bread and butter pickles, wasabi pickles, picnic relish, or any of hundreds of recipes for cucumbers. If you love jam, head to the farmers' market to see what bounty awaits. Don't be afraid to change direction based on the opportunities that present themselves. We often begin the growing season with a folder of recipes, a basket of seed packets, and heads full of big ideas. At the end of the summer, our pantry hardly ever looks the way we envisioned, but it is full of things we love and grew. So start there!

TIP 10: *Buy fruits and vegetables in season*

● You can buy almost any fruit or vegetable any time of year if you look hard enough and are willing to pay the price. Blueberries from Chile are available in January. Greenhouse-grown cucumbers are available in May. But produce is cheapest, and often best, when it is abundant and local, so it makes sense to buy foods when they are in season where you live. You'll pay less and also be able to pick the highest-quality produce. See the season-by-season guide to produce on the next page.

Season-By-Season Produce Guide

Spring

Apricots
Radishes
Ramps
Scallions
Artichokes
Asparagus
Beets
Fennel
Peas
Pea Pods
Snow Peas
Spinach
Swiss Chard
Vidalia Onions
Strawberries
Blueberries
Cherries
Herbs

Summer

Herbs
Eggplant
Melons
Nectarines
Peppers
Squash
Chili peppers
Corn
Cucumbers
Green Beans
Lima Beans
Okra

Tomatillos
Tomatoes
Edamame
Grapes
Okra
Onions
Pears
Zucchini
Apples
Blackberries
Cherries
Figs
Plums
Rhubarb
Blueberries
Currants

Fall

Rhubarb
Plums
Apples
Acorn Squash
Artichokes
Beets
Broccoli
Broccoli Raab
Brussels Sprouts
Cabbage
Celery
Cauliflower
Chili peppers
Cranberries
Edamame

Daikon Radish
Ginger
Bell peppers
Pumpkin
Sweet Potatoes
Swiss Chard
Turnips
Winter Squash
Grapes
Green Beans
Horseradish
Kale
Kohlrabi
Limes
Okra
Onions
Pears
Potatoes
Zucchini
Figs
Herbs

Winter

Brussels Sprouts
Cauliflower
Fennel
Kale
Parsnips
Mustard Greens
Turnips
Rutabagas
Citrus Fruits

TIP 11: *Use the best, ripest, and most perfect produce you can find*

⬤ If your passion is food, then you already know the thrill of finding the ripest and most beautiful heirloom tomatoes, the most succulent summer peaches, or the most perfect baby artichokes. You may be guilty of having done a little happy dance in the specialty market at seeing that fig vinegar you read about in last month's *Food and Wine* magazine. Or maybe your friends know your eyes will light up if you receive a bouquet of fresh dill. This passion for good food will serve you well in preserving because you already know what the best chefs know: Good food starts with good ingredients and great food starts with the very best ingredients.

The importance of the best, most mature, and perfect produce is magnified when your project involves preserving and storing. Excellent produce will increase your chances of an excellent product. Fruits and vegetables that are overripe, a bit underripe, bruised, or somewhat wormy—the seconds of the produce market—will not improve by being stuffed into jars, sitting in a dehydrator for hours, or lingering in your root cellar for 6 months. You may have saved a bit of money and have food on the shelves, but it won't be the best food or even food you even really want to eat or serve your family. So don't make do.

Make finding the best produce part of the preserving process. If your plan is to make apricot jelly but the apricots have seen better days yet the strawberries are luscious, then change the plan and make strawberry jam instead. If you can't find blueberries at one grocery store, go to another store or a farmers' market or hunt down a pick-your-own farm. This is the time to channel your inner perfectionist.

TIP 12: Know the Dirty Dozen ™ and the Clean Fifteen ™ of produce

Organic produce can be more expensive than conventionally grown produce, particularly if you're buying in large quantities for preserving. If you're trying to reduce your exposure to pesticides but are also working on a budget, it helps to prioritize by knowing which fruits and vegetables you should pay extra for to get organic (the Dirty Dozen) and which conventional produce is farmed in a fairly healthy and environment-friendly manner (the Clean Fifteen).

The Environmental Working Group (EWG) tracks the use of pesticides in produce and regularly updates a list of the fruits and vegetables with the heaviest concentrations of pesticides. They call the conventional produce to avoid the Dirty Dozen—apples, celery, cherry tomatoes, cucumbers, grapes, hot peppers, imported nectarines, peaches, potatoes, spinach, strawberries, and sweet bell peppers. The Clean Fifteen includes asparagus, avocados, cabbage, cantaloupe, sweet corn, eggplant, grapefruit, kiwis, mangoes, mushrooms, onions, papayas, pineapples, frozen sweet peas, and sweet potatoes. The most up-to-date list can be found on the EWG's website, www.ewg.org.

TIP 13: *Pay attention to the variety of produce you choose*

Not all tomatoes are alike. Neither are all cucumbers or all melons. Some varieties of vegetables and fruits are better for freezing, while others are better for canning. Some produce, such as alpine strawberries, should just be eaten fresh because their quality is lost in processing. Adding another layer of complexity to your choices is that some fruit and vegetable varieties are better suited for making certain types of foods. San Marzano tomatoes, for example, are paste tomatoes and better suited for making hearty marinara sauces and ketchups than for canning whole. So for the best results, do a bit of research on varieties that will work best for your recipe before heading to the store or farmers' market for your produce.

TIP 14: *Select wax-free produce*

Grocery stores routinely treat produce, such as cucumbers and apples, with edible waxes to slow moisture evaporation while the produce is on display. The problem for home preservers is that these products also prevent syrups, brines, and other fluids from thoroughly penetrating the skin and peels during the preserving process. Because these waxes cannot be effectively removed by washing or scrubbing, select wax-free produce or plan to peel products that have been treated. You can usually recognize treated produce by the unnaturally shiny appearance or by gently scraping your finger along the peel or skin to see if it feels waxy or oily. If you're in doubt, ask your store's produce manager if it has been treated.

TIP 15: *Make a day of produce picking at local pick-your-own farms*

You can save money on produce and still get the best and freshest available by picking your own strawberries, blueberries, or other produce at one of the many pick-your-own fruit and vegetable farms. These farms usually specialize in just one or a handful of crops and may only be open when the crops are mature and ready for picking. As a result, some farms may only be open for 2 or 3 weeks a year and only offer strawberries or blueberries, for example, and not have the kind of selection you would expect at the farmers' market. You will need to keep your eyes open for ready-to-pick signs or get on a farm's email alert list to know when to plan your picking trip.

When you head to the farm, take along snacks, hand towels, and plenty of water to drink. Wear a hat, sunscreen, and old clothes and shoes you don't mind getting muddy or torn. Bring your own shallow boxes or trays to hold fruit two or three layers deep. Berries piled into a deep bucket can easily get crushed and bruised. Check in at the entrance when you arrive to find out how the farm charges for their produce. Some charge by container size and others by weight or count. Practice good farm etiquette by leaving pets at home, taking care not to step on or otherwise damage plants, and keeping any nibbling to just a taste. After all, this is the farmer's product to sell, not a buffet! Finally, be prepared to pay cash since many farms are cash-only businesses.

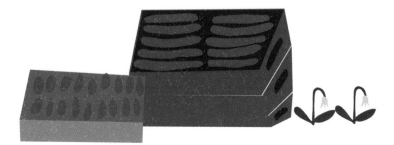

TIP 16: *Know how much produce you will need*

🌀 Some recipes will tell you how many beets you'll need to make 3 pints of pickles or how many pounds of blackberries will make six ½-pint jars of jam. Not all recipes are that detailed though. It helps to know more specifically how much you will need when buying produce so that you don't over- or underpick or buy. When in doubt, find a recipe for a similar processing method that includes the approximate processed yield. There are also suggested yield tables on the Internet. Of course, the best reference is the one you provide yourself and from your own experience. After you have made the recipe, make a note of how much produce you used and the final yield. It may vary a bit from batch to batch, but you'll have a better guideline for next time.

TIP 17: *Get a steady supply of fresh produce by joining a CSA*

🌀 Another option for fresh produce that is becoming increasingly available in many areas is community supported agriculture (usually referred to by its acronym, CSA). It's a long name for a simple concept. You purchase a share or shares from a local farmer who then delivers or makes available for pickup your portion of the farm's produce on a regular basis—usually once a week. There are no guarantees of what produce or how much you will get since you share in the farm's disasters, such as drought and deer damage. But you also share in the bounty. (Think zucchini. Lots of zucchini.) Some CSAs offer shares of eggs and meat products in addition to fruits, vegetables, and herbs for an extra fee. You'll need to sign up before the harvest season begins, usually in February or March, to secure your subscription.

TIP 18: *Know how to wash vegetables and fruits*

Before washing fruits and vegetables, remove outer leaves where most of the dirt and pesticide residues reside. Some produce, such as leeks, which have lots of nooks and crannies for sand and dirt to hide in, should be soaked briefly before rinsing. You may need to change the soaking water three or four times to clean them thoroughly. Use a scrub brush and rinse well in cool running tap water. One exception is mushrooms. Mushrooms should not be washed or rinsed. Clean mushrooms carefully with a damp cloth. If they are exceptionally dirty, give them a quick swish in cool water.

TIP 19: *Skip the produce-cleaning sprays*

Grocery stores and even health food stores sell special cleaning sprays for washing fruits and vegetables. There are also baking soda and vinegar recipes circulating on the Internet for homemade produce cleaning solutions. However, there is no evidence that these products are any more effective than washing in plenty of plain, cool tap water to remove dirt and residue. And if you don't thoroughly rinse after using them, you're just adding to the residues you don't want to eat.

TIP 20: *Handle hot peppers with care*

The capsaicin that makes peppers hot stays on hands and fingers even after you have washed them. It can be extremely painful to be reminded of having chopped hot peppers when you rub your eye or take out your contact lenses at night! Always use rubber gloves when handling hot peppers. In a pinch, you can put your hands in plastic bags to avoid touching peppers while washing and slicing. Cooks in the know even use plastic bags when picking out hot peppers at the store or market. It only takes a little bit of the capsaicin in your eyes to make a believer out of you.

GET ORGANIZED

TIP 21: *Outfit your kitchen*

⬤ If you haven't done any home preserving before, you may find there are lots of things you need now or will eventually want. Home preserving calls for many gadgets and much specialized equipment. To be sure, some gadgets are optional conveniences, but some are necessary equipment.

Consider what projects you plan to undertake and begin your hunting and gathering early so you have everything you need before you get started. If you are unsure of your commitment to make marmalade or dry fruit leathers more than once, then borrow what you need from friends and family. A list of suggested equipment is provided on pages 283–284 to get you started, but make sure you read your recipe thoroughly.

TIP 22: *Know about and practice mise en place*

● French chefs have a wonderful phrase that governs an approach to any cooking project—*mise en place* (pronounced MEEZ-ahn-plahs). It means "putting in place" and refers to how you prepare for your work in the kitchen. It describes not just what you do during the cooking project, but also your preparations before you peel the first carrot or turn on the first burner.

All ingredients should be measured out and their original containers stored back in the pantry or refrigerator. All produce should be prepared, including any washing, chopping, or peeling. The equipment you need should be nearby, clean, and ready. Knives should be sharp. You should, of course, have become very familiar with the recipe before getting started.

Frankly, getting into the habit of practicing mise en place will make your kitchen work less stressful and prone to error. Instead of last-minute scrambling for that double boiler at the back of the cabinet, you can focus on what you are cooking, the smells, sights, and sounds that indicate proper seasoning, whether your food is not quite ready, in danger of being overcooked, or a thousand other things. But even more important, the mise en place habit will make your work much more enjoyable.

Invest in sets of tiny bowls that can hold small amounts of measured ingredients. Set aside prep work time the day before your project for chopping and peeling that requires extra time. Clear your countertops and workspaces of clutter so that you can work calmly and efficiently.

TIP 23: *Set up a climate-controlled and efficient storage area*

⬤ If you plan to do a significant amount of canning, drying, or fermenting, consider how and where you plan to store the food for the weeks and months before it is consumed. Both canned and dry foods should be kept in a dark, dry, and cool, but not freezing, storage area. Shelves that are near toasters, ovens, or other heat-producing appliances are not suitable for food storage. Neither is garage storage, where temperatures can plummet. Moisture and humidity in utility rooms or damp basements can corrode or rust metal lids and compromise seals. Foods stored in areas that are too warm can spoil as bacteria reactivate at warm temperatures. Foods that freeze expand and can break glass jars and seals.

Those magazine and Internet photos of kitchen shelves lined with jars of canned goods are mouthwatering, but they aren't practical for long-term storage. Any foods stored in clear jars, bags, or other containers should also be stored in a dark area. It goes without saying that storage areas should be pest-free. Take precautions by putting dried foods in critter-proof containers.

TIP 24: *Organize your food storage*

⬤ Take care to organize your food products in ways that make sense for how you cook. Most people organize by food groups (vegetables, condiments, etc.) and then by food types within those groups (corn, beans, peaches, etc.). Other people organize foods so the most frequently used items are most accessible and can be found quickly without a search party.

Make a system that works for you and the way you cook. Labels on shelves can clearly identify your organization method and remind others where everything goes. Clear labels also can help identify the contents of pest-proof containers that hold bags of dried goods.

TIP 25: Investigate food rotation systems for large-scale food storage

● If you have room and plan on large-scale food storage, look into food rotation systems. Commercially sold food rotation systems are largely designed for foods in metal cans that can be stored on their sides and automatically roll to the front of the shelves as products are removed. Foods canned in jars should be stored upright, so look into alternatives that work for the home preserver.

If you are a skilled woodworker, you can craft a food storage system yourself with trays that glide out, allowing you to stock newer foods in the rear. A budget-friendly alternative for those of us who never took wood shop in school is to keep the original canning jar boxes to use as makeshift drawers or store-bought shelves.

TIP 26: Keep an inventory of stored foods

● It's easy to forget about food you squirreled away 6 months ago. Keep a running inventory of your stored food in a handy place where you can consult what foods you have available before menu planning or grocery shopping. Inventories can be kept on clipboards or in notebooks. There are general as well as specialized computer programs and apps that can be used to keep track of your food inventory. Some can even be accessed on your cell phone, if needed, when you are out shopping and need to see what items are running low.

TIP 27: *Regularly inspect and rotate stored food*

● Despite all the precautions you take to preserve your food properly, things can still go wrong. A jam jar lid seal can seep. Mice can feast on your dried trail mix. And just when you need a jar of tomatoes, you find that someone used the last jar a week ago. Head off problems before they escalate by regularly inspecting food you have stored. Look for problems such as broken seals, pantry pests, or moisture accumulating inside dried food packaging. Rotate older foods to the front or to the kitchen pantry so they can be remembered—and used—before their shelf life expires. Also inspect the storage area for signs of moisture, mouse droppings, or other problems that could affect the food you worked so hard to preserve.

TIP 28: *Have plenty of clean towels and rags handy*

● There is a lot of water involved with any type of preserving project. Produce must be washed and dried. Jars invariably drip water when they are removed from the hot water canner after sterilizing and processing. There will be spills. Be prepared for the inevitable drips and leaks by having stacks of fresh, clean towels, old T-shirts, and rags on standby. Always skip the fabric softener and scented dryer sheets for kitchen linens.

TIP 29: *Keep preserving in winter*

● You can continue stocking away home preserves even when there is snow on the ground. There are many delicious recipes for preserves made from fruit juice concentrates, canned vegetables, and even wine or cider. Some fruits are plentiful and ready for winter use, including lemons, limes, and oranges, to make luscious curds and citrus marmalades. Winter is also a great time to store dried foods for spring camping trips since the humidity is low, facilitating faster drying.

TIP 30: Have a checklist and workflow plan

Food preserving always involves certain steps, none of which should be skipped. It might help to have a checklist to follow for your workflow. Your canning workflow, for example, might be: inspect and wash jars, prepare food, sterilize jars, heat lids, fill jars, clean rims and place on lids and rings, process in the canner, remove, cool, check for seal, label, and store.

If your kitchen is large enough, you can arrange the food preparation and processing equipment into stations like an assembly line. If you're working in a smaller space, it may be easier and feel less chaotic to complete washing, peeling, and other food preparations before hauling out the jars and other equipment. Or you may want to have washed and inspected the jars and have them waiting on a tray in another room while you prepare the food and before sterilizing. Some jobs can be done the day or night before actual processing. Considering your space limitations and project, thinking through a workflow plan can help you feel less rushed—and also less likely to forget a step along the way.

TIP 31: Don't be afraid

Once you've read through all the material about methods, processes, steps, safety, and things that can go wrong, home preserving projects might start to feel a little high on the scary scale. But home food preserving is not like charting a course to Mars. People have canned, dried, fermented, and smoked foods successfully for generations. Yes, there are rules and steps to follow, but they are not complicated rules and steps. After you have a couple of successful projects under your belt, you'll wonder why you were concerned in the first place. So relax. Take one small project. Take your time and follow the instructions from start to finish. Evaluate your work and do another project. It's that simple!

DO NO HARM: SAFETY FIRST

TIP 32: Respect the Danger Zone

Throughout the tips in this book you'll see repeated references to temperatures and safety. There is a well-established zone, the Danger Zone, at which protein-rich foods are most vulnerable to attack by bacteria, yeasts, and molds that are in the environment or already present on the surface or inside the food. Between 40 and 140°F (4–60°C) these microorganisms can grow and multiply at an alarming rate. The rule-of-thumb is that meats, but also cooked foods such as casseroles, cooked beans—almost anything—should not remain within the Danger Zone for more than 2 hours.

TIP 33: Be clean

The foods you preserve will only be as clean and safe as your hands, your kitchen, the equipment, and the foods you choose. Taking steps to eliminate harmful microorganisms is a combination of common sense and following directions.

Wash your hands thoroughly and frequently, particularly when you leave the kitchen or touch pets or dirty surfaces. Avoid cross-contamination by having separate cutting boards for meats and produce. Clean knives, cutting boards, and other equipment after each use with hot, soapy water. Sanitize counters, sinks, and drains with hot, soapy water or a sanitizing spray. When working on a major kitchen project, replace kitchen towels and wash cloths frequently or use paper towels. If you use a non-metallic kitchen sponge, put it in the microwave on high for 2 minutes. Be particularly vigilant when working with raw meats.

TIP 34: Don't forget to clean sinks and drains

Your kitchen sink and drain are among the most bacteria-ridden places in your home. A research study by the Hygiene Council found that the average kitchen drain has 567,845 bacteria per square inch. The sink near the drain has 13,227 bacteria per square inch. And your kitchen sponge or washcloth? 134,630 bacteria per square inch.

Scour kitchen sinks, including faucets, drains, and stoppers daily with a sanitizing cleanser. Scrub work surfaces with soap and water and spray with a disinfecting spray. And don't forget your dishwasher. Run it empty on the sanitizing cycle on a regular basis or regularly wipe it down according to the manufacturer's instructions.

TIP 35: Make your own sanitizing spray

Hot, soapy water is effective cleanup for most projects. But a sanitizing spray will help kill lingering bacteria you can't see. You can make your own sanitizing spray by mixing ¾tsp (4ml) household bleach and 2 pints (1L) water in a spray bottle.

CANNING

There is science behind safe and successful canning, such as understanding pH, safe canning practices, and appropriate storage. Thankfully, it is not overly complicated science. Once the basics are understood, the most gratifying parts of canning are the creativity and the many possibilities of lining your pantry shelves with your own luscious jams, piquant pickles, and sweet and savory sauces. It's the perfect combination of art and science.

CANNING BASICS

TIP 36: *For safety, rely on USDA-tested methods and proven recipes*

Home food preserving isn't complex, but there are safe and unsafe practices and recipes. Some of them may surprise you! In fact, the United States Department of Agriculture's Department National Center for Home Food Preservation conducted surveys that revealed that a large percentage of home food preservers were using unsafe preserving methods, potentially putting themselves and their families at risk of food poisoning.

Recipes intended for general cooking were not intended for and should not be used for canning. Not even all canning recipes you can find on the Internet are necessarily safe. (Nor are all the methods you can find, for that matter.)

To best evaluate a recipe or practice, home preservers should become familiar with and follow recommended safety practices for all home food preserving projects. Utilizing laboratory development, testing, and critical literature reviews, the Center has developed extensive recommendations for the safe preservation of foods through canning, freezing, drying, fermenting, and pickling, as well as curing and smoking. They are all free and available online from the National Center for Home Food Preservation (http://nchfp.uga.edu).

TIP 37: *Think practically about the recipe you choose to use*

You have many choices when it comes to selecting the recipe you want to use for your canning projects. It may feel like too many. How do you go about picking one that will work for you and make the effort worthwhile? The first four considerations should be practical ones.

First, do you have or can you borrow the equipment you will need to make the recipe safely? Some foods must be processed in a pressure canner. If you don't have one you can still make the recipe, but you will need to refrigerate the food and use it within a few days rather than processing it for shelf storage. The second question is also a practical one and is about time. Do you have enough of it? Some canning projects can take many hours, particularly those that involve several hours of pressure processing, while other projects, such as a small-batch jam-making recipe, can be made in less than an hour. Third, is the produce you want to use in season and available? Consult the list on page 19 or peruse farmers' markets or grocery stores to check availability. Fourth, is the recipe safe? Recipes developed by the National Center for Home Food Preservation are a great place for beginners to start, but you don't have to be limited to those. As long as you are familiar with and consult resources about safe canning practices, you can evaluate the safety of most recipes.

TIP 38: *Think about the quality and flavors of the recipe you are considering*

⚫ Once the practical considerations of selecting a recipe are squared away, you can turn your attention to the fun stuff—taste. If you haven't made a recipe before, how do you know if you will like it? Beyond the obvious fact that you may hate apricots or love anything that includes cardamom, there are some guidelines that can help.

First, consider recipes from cooks that you know and that have been developed by chefs. Ask people you know who are canners to recommend a recipe you might like. (They will probably fall all over themselves to help you out. "Oh, thank goodness! Another canner!") Thanks to the food television networks, nearly everyone can name a famous chef or twelve. If there is a particular chef whose style of cooking and use of flavors appeals to you, check to see if they have developed any recipes for use in canning. Many chefs have, particularly now that pickles, chutneys, and specialty jams are all the rage in posh restaurants.

Other considerations are, of course, ingredients. The ingredients must be available, obviously, but some ingredients just work better together than others. Browsing specialty food catalogs will give you some ideas of flavor combinations you hadn't considered but that might be very appealing. One specialty jam company makes an Adriatic fig and tomato jam. Another makes a habanero and blackberry jam. You don't have to stick with single-ingredient preserves. Finally, consider the complexity, not just of the recipe, but of the flavors. Recipes that have just a few ingredients can be delightfully simple and pure, but recipes that have more ingredients are likely to have a greater depth of complexity and flavor.

TIP 39: *Learn about the acidity of produce*

⚫ A combination of heat and acid is needed in canning to prohibit the growth of harmful bacteria. Heat is provided by the canner. Acid is naturally occurring in the food and is measured using the pH scale, from 1, the most acid, to 14, the most alkali (least acid). The pH level of a food determines the temperature needed to destroy harmful bacteria, and thus dictates what method must be used in canning.

Foods with an acidity level of 4.6 or lower are considered acidic foods and can be safely processed in a hot-water bath canner. Lower acid foods—foods with an acidity level above 4.6—must be processed in a pressure canner at a temperature of 240°F (116°C) at 10lb of pressure. Processing times will depend on the degree of acidity, the density of the food, jar size, and other variables. For a general guide on processing method, refer to the illustration.

Acidity chart of common produce

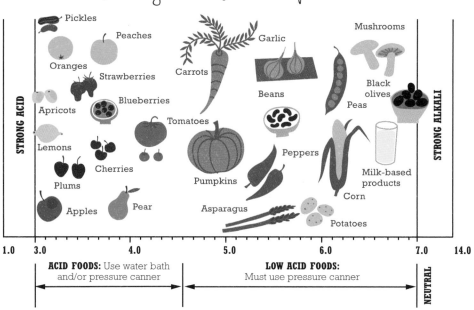

TIP 40: *Know that acidity levels can be altered in some foods*

The acidity level of some foods can be altered with the addition of acids such as lemon juice, citric acid, or vinegar, making them safe for processing in a hot-water bath canner. Although tomatoes are generally thought of as a high-acid food, many tomatoes do not contain enough acid for safe hot-water bath processing. Similarly, figs have a pH level just above 4.6. But with the addition of the right amount of acid, both figs and tomatoes can be safely processed in a hot-water bath canner. Refer to recipes and tested guidelines for the appropriate measures and combinations for safe processing. Remember never to reduce or omit the acids in a recipe. They serve an important safety function.

TIP 41: *Measure accurately*

Carpenters and seamstresses have the expression, "Measure twice. Cut once." There may not be an equivalent expression for cooking, but it's a useful idea and one that is particularly important in food preserving. Because safety depends on the right ratio of salt to water in brining and the precise measurement of lemon juice added to tomatoes in canning, for example, measuring accurately is critical.

When measuring liquids, use clear glass or plastic measuring cups that allow you to gauge the measure at eye level. Chefs usually measure dry ingredients by weight on a precise kitchen scale. Most of the recipes home cooks use don't have weight equivalents, but you can improve your measuring precision by spooning in dry ingredients and leveling the measuring cup with a knife. Level dry ingredients on your measuring spoons as well. Never fill a measuring cup by scooping into the flour crock because that will pack the flour in too tightly, putting too much flour into your recipe. And, of course, measure time precisely as well, particularly in canning processing.

TIP 42: *Adjust processing time for your altitude*

🍇 Since water boils at a lower temperature and isn't as hot at boiling point in higher altitudes, processing times must be adjusted accordingly for safe processing. Check with your county agricultural extension agent or soil conservation service if you need help determining the elevation of your area. See page 285 for processing adjustment information or consult one of the handy online calculators for determining processing time. It's also a good idea to make a habit of jotting down on each recipe you use the processing time adjustments for your altitude. It will help you avoid having to do the calculation the next time you use the recipe.

TIP 43: *Don't can like your grandma*

🍇 No offense to your grandma (or grandpa!), but some of the canning methods used in the past should stay in the past. Leaving the lid off of a hot-water bath canner during processing, called open kettle canning, doesn't keep the temperature high enough or stable enough. Sealing jam and jelly jars with a layer of melted paraffin used to be a standard, accepted practice. Now, research has shown that paraffin doesn't create the airproof seal needed for safe storage. If you're using an old recipe that calls for a paraffin seal, know that you'll need to modify the processing and sealing to update it to current safety methods.

TIP 44: *Don't use unproven "modern" canning methods either*

Every new appliance seems to be ushered in with unconventional ideas for using them. Just say no to unproven canning methods that use the microwave, dishwasher, or slow cooker. Steam canners are available, but despite claims by manufacturers, the safety of canning with steam is still being researched and is as-yet unproven.

The Internet is also home to some extremely risky advice, including suggestions to try the so-called "dry canning" method, which uses oxygen-absorbing packets to create a vacuum seal in jars. Don't be misled by the name. Dry canning is not a safe canning alternative. For canning, stick with what is proven to be safe—hot-water bath canners and pressure canners, depending on the acidity level of the food.

TIP 45: *Don't use the flip and seal method*

Some older canning books will suggest that you flip processed jars upside down to create an airtight barrier along the lid for sealing. The sealing compound on modern canning lids makes this unnecessary. It also makes it possible for tiny amounts of liquid to work through a not-quite-set seal and create a leak, leading to premature spoilage. Always leave jars upright during cooling and storage.

TIP 46: *Beware of oven processing*

⬤ Some well-known European chefs advocate processing jars in the oven in lieu of water bath or pressure canning. The reasoning is that jars kept in a hot oven for long enough will reach the right temperature for safe preserving. Unfortunately, oven temperatures vary and the dry oven air doesn't conduct heat as efficiently as a hot-water bath canner that surrounds the jars in boiling water. Until oven processing methods are tested and approved, stick with USDA-recommended processing methods.

TIP 47: *Take extra safety precautions when handling raw meats*

⬤ Raw meats, including poultry, are high in moisture and protein, the type of environment where disease-causing microorganisms can thrive. Whenever you handle meats, whether it is for preserving or for making dinner, always follow safe handling guidelines. Keep raw meats refrigerated at below 40°F (4°C) Use recommended thawing procedures rather than thawing frozen meats at room temperature. Always marinate meats in the refrigerator rather than on the countertop. Take steps to avoid cross-contamination by keeping a cutting board that is only used for cutting raw meats—never for vegetables, cheese, or other foods. Wash hands thoroughly after handling raw meat and carefully wash countertops, cutting boards, and utensils that come into contact with them. Use a sanitizing spray for an extra measure of safety.

TIP 48: *Use canned foods within a year*

⚫ Stored in a cool, dry place, canned goods will be safe to eat for about a year. If canned goods are exposed to light or to heat from a furnace, hot plumbing pipes, or household appliances, they will deteriorate more quickly and should be consumed sooner. Make sure the processing date is indicated on the label so you know when your home-preserved food is past its recommended use-by date.

TIP 49: *Know how to identify signs of spoilage*

⚫ Before eating any canned product, take a moment to observe the container and contents. There are some obvious warning signs that a canned product has spoiled and should not be eaten by people or animals. Seeping of any sort, bulging lids, bubbling or mold around the seal or visible in the contents, cloudy-, yeasty-, spongy-, or shriveled-looking foods, or food with an unnatural color are warning signs that should not be ignored.

If your canned product looks clean and safe on the outside, take a moment after opening for another inspection. If the container spurts liquid when it opens, it is a sign of spoilage, as are musty odors and any other indications of mold, slime, or suspicious texture. Never taste a suspicious food to test for spoilage!

TIP 50: *Safely dispose of spoiled products*

Suspicious food products could potentially contain the *C. botulinum* toxin. If ingested, this toxin can affect nerves, cause paralysis and even death. Foodborne botulism is rare but is serious enough that you should take any signs of spoilage seriously and dispose of foods safely.

If you have a product you suspect has spoiled, wear gloves and an apron or towel that can be machine washed. Take care to avoid splashing spoiled contents or allowing the contents to come into contact with your skin. Do not dispose of spoiled food in garbage disposals, in the yard, woods, or down the toilet. Place the spoiled food and container in a sealable plastic bag. Wrap this bag in another plastic bag and wrap tightly with tape. Place the sealed container in the non-recyclable trash outside the house, making sure that the garbage can lid is sealed so pets and wildlife cannot get in. Discard rags, gloves, or other items that may have come into contact with the spoiled food. Wash your hands thoroughly with soap and water. Treat countertops and any other areas with hot, soapy water or a sanitizing spray.

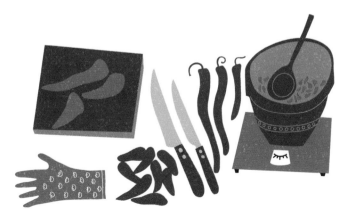

TIP 51: *Know what not to worry about*

Not every bubble and speck is something to worry about. Marinara sauce that has separated into red and watery layers and cherries bobbing at the top of the canning jar may look worrisome, but by itself, floating fruit or separated sauces are not dangerous. There could be many causes for this aesthetic problem, including using fruit that is too ripe, packing too loosely, raw packing, or even overprocessing. Next time you use the recipe, review your cooking, packing, and processing procedures. In the meantime, just stir the foods before heating and serving.

Likewise, bubbles that you see at the top of the jars of recently processed foods are not early signs of spoilage. Air bubbles that were trapped in the food or escaping from the cell structure are just working their way to the top of the jar. Sometimes you may notice small black specks on the lids of canned tomatoes or other foods. These are tannins in the food or hydrogen sulfides that form as a by-product of the process and also are perfectly harmless.

TIP 52: *Know that you're not finished when you think you're finished*

After the jars are processed and you have washed and dried the equipment, you're not really finished. There are a few more to-do items that the canning books don't stress in the workflow descriptions. After the jars have cooled and you have tested the seals, wipe or gently wash the outside of the jars to remove any remaining food residue. Label the jars with the contents and the processing date. Move them to the designated storage space. And finally, sit down with your kitchen notebook and make notes about your project, including the source of the recipe and ingredients, yield, dates, and active/passive work time.

JARS AND LIDS

TIP 53: *Size matters when selecting canning jars*

Canning recipes specify the size jar for the recipe based on the prescribed processing time. Larger jars require a longer processing time in order to bring the contents to a temperature needed for safety. If your recipe doesn't provide the processing time for larger jars, then stick with the jar size the recipe indicates. It is usually safe to use smaller jars, but you risk overheating the jar contents, which can impact texture and quality.

TIP 54: *Use wide-mouth jars for canning larger foods*

Canning jars come in regular and wide-mouth varieties. Choose the wide-mouth jars for canning larger foods, such as whole tomatoes and peaches. It makes the packing process easier. It's also easier to remove the contents from the jar when it comes time to serve.

TIP 55: *Save the boxes for storing*

Since you can reuse canning jars and rings, keep the original packing box to store jars after you empty them. Storing in sectioned boxes is more organized, cleaner, and less dangerous than having dozens of empty glass jars jumbled on a shelf in the basement.

TIP 56: *Don't repurpose jars for canning*

● Canning jars are made of clear tempered glass, which makes them safe for processing in high heat. Repurposed jars that once held store-bought foods are not tempered and so are not safe for hot-water bath or pressure cooking. They are very likely to break or shatter when exposed to high heat during processing. Even if they don't break, the jar lids on repurposed jars are insufficient for proper sealing and storage and it is unlikely that you will be able to find canning lids to fit. Save mayonnaise, peanut butter, and other jars for other projects, such as crafts or holding office supplies.

TIP 57: *Clean and inspect jars and lids before canning*

● Taking an inventory of jars and lids is best done well before you begin your canning project. You'll need to confirm that you have the right number of jars of the size you need, and also enough new lids. Inspect each jar carefully for chips or cracks that could cause the jar to break in processing or create an imperfect seal. Never reuse lids because it is not sanitary and they may not seal completely. You can reuse the rings of two-part lid assemblies, but throw away any rings that are rusted or otherwise damaged. Thoroughly wash and dry the jars and lids you plan to use. Make sure jars are rinsed well so that any lingering soapy film will not affect food taste.

TIP 58: *Remove scale, hard water film, and rust from jars before using*

● Your jars may not look new, but they should look as close to new as possible before you use them for your canning project. Carefully scour away any rust spots that may be left behind by jar lids and rings. If jars have scale or cloudy hard water deposits, soak them overnight in a mixture of 1 cup of vinegar and 1 gallon (3.8L) of water and then rewash and dry.

TIP 59: *Know the advantages and disadvantages of different lid types*

There are several different lid types offered by canning jar manufacturers. The lids recommended by the USDA are the two-part assembly with a flat lid and a separate screw ring to secure the lid in place while processing. These lids are treated with a sealing compound that softens when heated to create an airtight seal. Lids can be stored and used for up to five years after manufacture, but it is better to purchase only the number of lids you will need for a project or season than to store lids. When in doubt, throw it out.

Some manufacturers offer reusable lids or a single unit lid that also has a compound that, when softened in heat, works to create a seal. Other manufacturers make jars with glass lid and clamp assemblies. These jars are attractive but many home preservers report difficulty securing the clamps properly and a high seal failure rate. The USDA does not recommend these lid types. Jars made specifically for freezing and jars with clamps and rubber seals are not appropriate for canning.

TIP 60: *After processing, remove rings—at least temporarily*

After processing and cooling, lid rings are no longer necessary and should be removed so that they do not rust and corrode in storage. If you still plan to store jars with rings in place, cool the jars for 24 hours and then remove the rings for another few hours so that any moisture that has accumulated under the rings can evaporate.

TIP 61: *Do not use extra-large canning jars*

⚫ Manufacturers still offer canning jars in 3- and 5-pint (1.4 and 1.9L) sizes. These extra-large sizes are no longer recommended for hot-water bath or pressure canning because the processing times necessary to heat foods to the center of the jar are so long they result in overprocessing foods on the outer part of the jar, damaging flavor, color, and texture. Save those large jars for storing dried fruit and vegetables.

TIP 62: *Use BPA-free canning lids*

⚫ Until recently, most lids in the two-piece canning lid and ring assemblies available in the United States contained BPA (Bisphenol A), a synthetic estrogen that hardens plastic and inhibits metal from rusting. BPA is widely found in canned and plastic products, but it's a concern because food that comes into contact with BPA absorbs the chemical and it goes into the body when ingested. Manufacturers are aware of the growing public outcry about the safety of our foods and now some manufacturers have reformulated their canning lids to be BPA-free. Read labels carefully and choose lids you know are free of BPA.

TIP 63: *Use dissolvable labels on your jars*

⚫ If you like the look of a nice, tidy label on a jar but don't fancy having to scrape it off with your fingernail to reuse the jar again later, investigate the new dissolvable labels. These labels are made to stick securely on jars during storage and use and then dissolve during hand or dishwasher washing.

CANNERS AND EQUIPMENT

TIP 64: *Selecting a hot-water bath canner*

⑨ A hot-water bath canner is a fairly simple piece of equipment—a large aluminum or porcelain-covered steel pot fitted with a jar rack and a lid. The jar rack is needed to keep jars in place while processing so they don't knock against each other and break. The rack also ensures that hot water can completely circulate around the jars during processing.

Hot-water bath canners are widely available at discount retailers, hardware stores, and sometimes in grocery or drug stores. Choose a canner that is deep enough to fill to at least 1 in (2.5cm) of water above the jars, so the larger the jars you plan to use, the deeper your canner needs to be. If you have a large enough stockpot with a lid, you can buy a jar rack separately and it'll serve quite nicely as a hot-water bath canner.

TIP 65: *Select a pressure canner with the newer safety features*

● Modern pressure canners are light years ahead of old canners in terms of safety, so don't buy an old pressure canner at a garage sale thinking you're getting a good deal. It may not be safe and it may not be accurate either.

The pressure canner has the kettle and the lid, of course. Inside the kettle you should have a removable rack for holding jars. The lid will be tight-fitting and fasten down with clamps or with interlocking grooves and ridges. Some pressure canners have rubber gaskets around the lid.

Pressure canners come in several sizes, the most popular of which are the 16-quart (15.1L) and 22-quart (20.8L) sizes. Unlike with hot-water bath canners, you don't need to completely cover the jars with water since it is the pressurized heat inside the canner that will do the work. But only buy as large a canner as you'll need. The largest sizes allow you to stack jars in two levels, increasing efficiency for large processing projects, but also requiring more time to bring to a boil.

The controls are located on the lid and include a pressure gauge, a vent, and a safety valve or plug. There are two types of pressure gauge—dial gauges and weighted gauges—that regulate the pressure inside the canner. The vent on the lid allows air and steam to exhaust before processing time begins. This vent is closed with a petcock or weight to start the pressure. The safety valve or plug-in modern canners will automatically blow if the pressure gets too high. Pressure canners can be very expensive, so it pays to do your homework.

TIP 66: *If you have only one canner, pick a pressure canner*

You don't have to use the pressure controls on your pressure canner. If you only want to buy or have room for one canner, choose a pressure canner, which you can use as a hot-water bath canner too.

TIP 67: *How to work your pressure canner*

Working a pressure canner is actually quite simple once you get the hang of it. After loading, cover with the lid and secure. Turn on the heat and bring the water to a boil with the vent open. Steam must come from the vent for at least 7 minutes—10 minutes for larger canners—to ensure that there is enough steam inside the canner to begin processing. Only after this time has passed can you close the vent. After closing the vent, monitor the dial gauge and adjust the heat to keep it steady at the pressure specified in the recipe. Follow manufacturer instructions for calculating pressure on canners with weighted gauges. After the processing time, remove the canner from the heat and wait until the pressure drops to zero before slowly opening the vent. You can remove the lid after steam has stopped coming from the vent.

TIP 68: Take your pressure canner on a test drive

If you are new to pressure canning, take your pressure canner on a test drive without any jars for processing. Find a recipe that specifies processing time and pressure and see how your canner behaves on your stove. Let the canner vent and then close the vent to allow pressure to build. Experiment with the temperature controls to achieve a steady pressure indication on the gauge. Gas stoves are much easier to work with because the flame is immediately on/off or high/low with the turn of a dial. Electric stoves are slower to respond and so are trickier to work with. It may take some practice to get the feel of how to manage the controls to achieve a steady pressure.

TIP 69: Carry out pre-season and post-season pressure canner care

A pressure canner can be a big investment, so take steps to make sure it's in good shape for the next canning season and then store it properly during the months of non-use. The rubber gasket, if there is one, should be removed and washed in hot, sudsy water and dried before being replaced on the canner. Never wash rubber gaskets in the dishwasher because the drying cycle can dry out the rubber. Follow manufacturer instructions to remove and wash the air lock and perform any other regular maintenance your canner requires.

The inside of your canner may discolor and darken due to iron and minerals in the water, but this won't affect canner operation. If you want your canner to look shiny new, you can remove those deposits. Fill your canner up to two-thirds full. Add 1tsp of cream of tartar for each quart (1L) of water in the canner. Close the canner and heat to 15lb of pressure, then remove from the heat and allow it to sit for 2 hours before opening, washing, and drying.

TIP 70: Store your pressure canner the right way

🕮 Store your pressure canner in a box or in a sealed plastic bag to keep debris and excess moisture out. Fill the canner with clean paper towels to absorb any moisture and odors. Never seal the canner for storage. Instead, store the lid upside down on the canner.

TIP 71: Test your pressure canner gauge for accuracy

🕮 Pressure canners have weighted or dialed gauges for regulating the pressure during processing. Weighted gauges do not require testing, but the USDA recommends that dial gauges be checked annually for accuracy. Gauges that read high can result in underprocessing and unsafe food. Low readings can cause overprocessing, impacting food quality.

Some pressure canner manufacturers and local county agricultural extension service offices will test gauges for no charge or for a small fee. Pressure adjustments can be made if the gauge reads up to 2lb high or low. Gauges that differ by more than 2lb will need to be replaced.

TIP 72: Test out your hot-water bath canner to determine water level

🕮 If you're new to canning, you may not know how much water you need to add to your hot-water bath canner to ensure you have 1in (2.5cm) water level above the lids. Waiting until you're ready to process can mean you need to add water at the last minute, increasing the time jars filled with food are exposed to heat. Do this. With the canner rack and jars in place, fill the canner with water to 1–2in (2.5–5cm) above the jar tops, then remove the jars. The remaining water level is how much water you need to have in the canner when it's time for processing.

TIP 73: Buy—and use—a jar lifter and a lid lifter

Hoisting hot jars out of boiling water is serious business. They can feel amazingly heavy. Plus, they're slippery and awkward to get out of the canner. A jar lifter looks like large, rubberized tongs designed to fit securely around the neck of canning jars so they can be safely removed from the canner without slipping. A lid lifter looks like a little plastic stick with a magnet on the end. It's an inexpensive little gadget that makes fishing stuck-together disk lids out of hot water easier.

TIP 74: Lift jars by the jar neck and not the lid

When lifting hot jars out of the canner, use the jar lifter to securely grasp the jar around its glass neck and not the metal ring. Jars are not completely sealed at this point and squeezing the metal ring to lift the jar can allow air to get in and ruin the seal. For the same reason, lift jars straight up rather than at an angle.

TIP 75: Bring out the special equipment to save time

Crushing tomatoes for a smooth ketchup or plums for a silky sauce can take time to accomplish by hand. An immersion blender can be a real time saver, especially for large-scale projects. An immersion blender allows you to plunge the cutting/blending tool right into your cooking pot or bowl and move it around to process the food in place. Less high-tech but still effective is a hand-crank food mill to process produce into smooth sauce.

METHODS AND TECHNIQUES

TIP 76: *Understand the importance of processing*

● Canned foods that will not be stored in the refrigerator or freezer are processed for a prescribed amount of time in a hot-water bath or pressure canner. This is one of the most important parts of the canning process, so getting it right is imperative. Processing protects against bacteria, mold, and yeast that can make your food unsafe. During processing, the entire contents of the food packed in jars—not just the outer layer—must have time to reach a temperature high enough to kill those microorganisms.

The processing time is determined by the acidity and density of the food, the size of the jar, and other factors, such as added acids and sugars. Cutting corners by shaving a few minutes off of the processing time can result in jars that weren't heated all the way to the center, which can lead to spoilage and unsafe produce. On the other hand, overprocessing jars by adding an extra few minutes can cause your food to become mushy and discolored, and can kill lots of good vitamins. So, take note of processing and follow instructions to the letter.

TIP 77: *You may need to use distilled water*

● Tap water, particularly hard water and even some bottled water, can have high concentrations of minerals that can cause preserved foods made with water, such as brined pickles, to turn dark. If you have problems with pickles or other foods darkening when in storage, try using distilled water in the recipe next time.

TIP 78: Embrace small-batch canning

Back in the days when people canned to fill the pantry for winter, canning was a major production involving dozens of jars, about as many hours, and a small posse of workers. It was a marathon, exhausting event. Today, many recipes are for much smaller quantities—sometimes as few as two or three jars—and often take only as much time as it does to make dinner. Besides fitting better into busy schedules, you need smaller quantities of produce for small-batch canning. You can experiment with many more of the specialized recipes available in the numerous small-batch canning cookbooks that line the shelves of the local bookstore.

TIP 79: Fill your canner with hot water

Starting off with hot water reduces the amount of time it takes for all that water to come to a boil. This may seem elementary, but it's amazing how many people forget when there are several things going on at one time in the kitchen.

TIP 80: Use two burners

Most canning books will tell you to select a canner that is no more than 4in (10cm) in diameter larger than your burner. If your canner is larger than that or if you find that your water is taking too long to boil or come back to a boil once you have placed jars in for processing, try straddling the canning pot over two burners. Most canners are large enough to do this safely. Take care to ensure the burner closest to where you work is completely covered.

TIP 81: *Watch the clock*

Safe canning requires processing at boiling for specified times based on the food product, jar size, and altitude. This is not the time for guessing the time, so get a kitchen timer and use it. Don't begin timing the processing in canning until the water has come back to a full boil.

TIP 82: *Take steps to preserve texture and color of foods in canning*

Some foods that are canned and stored change in color and texture more than others. Foods such as apples and peaches, which have a tendency to brown, will benefit by the addition of ascorbic acid to preserve the color. Overripe fruits and fruits packaged in water or fruit juice will not maintain their color as well as fruits packed in sugar syrups. You can also prevent foods from darkening in the jar and changing texture by storing in a cool, dark location.

TIP 83: *Refrigerate produce you can't can immediately*

Produce for preserving should be at the peak of ripeness and flavor. Once it is picked though, produce immediately begins its decline—shriveling, becoming mushy, and losing color. Nutritional content also declines from the moment produce is picked. Factor this into your canning timetable. If you have to hold produce for a day or two before canning, refrigerate or store it in a cool, well-ventilated location. If your blueberries or strawberries begin to be more overripe than ripe, then plan on a strawberry shortcake for dinner and blueberries in your morning yogurt rather than investing time and effort into preserving sub-prime produce.

TIP 84: *Be extra cautious about baby food preparations*

⊛ Home-canning for baby food allows you greater control over the salt, sugars, and additives in your baby's diet. But there are limits to what you may safely can for consumption by babies. You certainly can't home-can all the products you see in baby jars in the grocery store. Never home-can meats or seafood for a baby's consumption. You can use whole or chunk vegetables, but purée them only at the point of serving the food. Since vegetables are low-acid foods, it is not safe to purée them before being canned because this would concentrate the foods, making it difficult to properly acidify or process safely. The same goes for purées of low-acid fruits, such as bananas, figs, pears, and mangoes. Also, use the smallest jars, tiny $\frac{1}{2}$-pint (0.24L) sizes, and follow all the recommended procedures and processing times precisely.

TIP 85: *Know when to use hot packing and cold packing*

⊛ There are two methods of packing jars: the hot pack and the cold pack methods. Most canning recipes will specify the packing method. Hot packing is used most often and involves cooking the food before packing it into jars along with the cooking liquid. Hot packing softens fruits and vegetables, allowing you to fit more into the jar. In cold packing, on the other hand, raw produce is put into the jars and hot liquid is poured over the produce. The processing time is usually longer so that the heat can penetrate to the center of the food, but cold packing allows you to more artfully arrange foods, such as asparagus and uncut green beans.

TIP 86: *Use your canner to sterilize jars*

Some canning instructions will call for sterilizing jars in boiling water before filling. You could set up another big pot of boiling water for the job, but if you are using a hot-water bath canner, you could also just use that! Place jars in the canner before you bring the water to a boil and while you are preparing your food. After 10 minutes, you can remove and fill the jars. This probably wouldn't work with pressure canners since they use less water than hot-water bath canners.

TIP 87: *Use a wide-mouth canning funnel*

Wide-mouth canning funnels make the job of filling jars faster and with fewer spills and splatters. It's not just a convenience. Clean jar rims are important to creating a good seal. You can find wide-mouth canning funnels at hardware stores and online.

TIP 88: *Fill jars on wax paper-lined baking pans*

There will inevitably be drips when you fill your jars. Lining jars up on a wax paper-lined baking pan makes cleanup easier. It also allows you to move jars more easily around your workspace.

TIP 89: *Leave an appropriate amount of headspace*

🍓 Most recipes will indicate the amount of space you should leave at the top of the jar. This is called headspace. Overfilling jars will result in seepage and an improper seal, not to mention that it will make a big mess! Underfilling jars will also result in an improper seal because not enough air can escape to create a vacuum. Over- or underfilling increases the risk of deterioration and spoilage. Headspace allows for the expansion of the food and air in the jar during processing to create a proper seal.

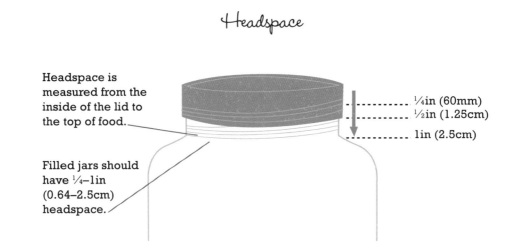

Headspace

Headspace is measured from the inside of the lid to the top of food.

Filled jars should have ¼–1in (0.64–2.5cm) headspace.

¼in (60mm)
½in (1.25cm)
1in (2.5cm)

TIP 90: *Get rid of air bubbles*

⊕ Bubbles allowed to stay in the jar are excess air. They can work their way to the top of the jar during storage and leave the contents at the top exposed to air, which will cause discoloration. After filling your jars and before securing lids, take a couple of minutes to examine the contents and work out any air bubbles that may be trapped among the food. There are special bubble-removing gadgets on the market, but you don't need them. A chopstick, ice cream stick, or other wooden or plastic stick or knife will do very nicely. Gently slide the knife along the inside edges of the jar and lightly press the preserves to allow air bubbles to escape. Repeat this process several times until all the air bubbles are released. Add more liquid, as needed, to adjust the headspace to the correct level.

TIP 91: *Learn the technique to reduce air bubbles*

⊕ Preserving pros have learned the tricks for making their work easier and more effective. One of those tricks is exactly how to fill a jar before processing to reduce air bubbles. Use a wide-mouth canning funnel to make filling cleaner and easier. Using a ladle, fill jars as close to the mouth as possible so that foods don't plop or splash and create more air bubbles. This technique doesn't avoid the need to remove air bubbles, but it does reduce their number.

TIP 92: Don't overtighten or re-tighten lids

⬢ Follow manufacturer instructions for the correct lid preparation. Most instructions call for you to carefully clean jar rims of any foods or juices and then to finger-tighten the lid into place, just securing the lid without screwing it down hard, which can cause breaking. "Finger-tighten" seems a bit too vague for a lot of people, so one manufacturer has created a gadget that will tighten the lid with just the right amount of torque.

Lids are treated with a compound that will soften and create a seal around the rim during processing, so re-tightening rings after processing is not needed, nor is it recommended.

TIP 93: Don't rush the cool-down of a pressure canner

⬢ Before pressure canner lids can be removed safely, the internal pressure must drop to zero. If you open the vent before then, the sudden change in pressure can also pull liquid from the jars or cause them to break, ruining all your hard work. Never use cold water to try to hasten the cool-down. If you rush this time, you will actually be shaving time off the processing.

TIP 94: Use a footstool if you need it

⬢ Canners are deep. Add the height of the stove, gallons of boiling water, and slippery wet jars and it can be a dangerous combination. If you are not very tall or if you just want some extra leverage to reach to the bottom of the canner for your jam jar, use a sturdy footstool so you can reach more easily and safely.

TIP 95: *A PING! is a good thing*

At some point when your jars are cooling you are likely to hear a series of distinctive PINGS! More than one beginning home preserver has run to call grandma or search the Internet to find out if he or she did something wrong. Good news! That ping you hear is the metal lid responding to the vacuum created inside the jar during processing. It is the sound of a successful seal! If you don't hear a ping, don't worry yet. Just wait and check for a seal later.

TIP 96: *Let jars rest for 24 hours*

After removing jars from the canner they need to rest and cool for the seal to completely set. Moving them around can interrupt this process and increase the chances that a seal will fail. Now is the time to practice some patience. Place the jars in a location where they can remain undisturbed.

TIP 97: *Check the seal and fix jars that fail to seal properly*

Close inspection will tell you if your canned goods have sealed properly. Properly sealed jars have a slight concave bend to the top of the metal lid that is caused by the vacuum created during processing. A lid that pops back up after you press down gently on it is not sealed. Failure to create a seal is usually caused by improper processing time, too much headspace in the jar, or a nick or chip in the jar rim. Boiling rather than heating or other improper handling of jar lids before processing can also cause failure.

Jars that fail to seal can be reprocessed within 24 hours. Inspect the jar to make sure it is free of imperfections. Use a new lid and a new jar, if necessary, and reprocess the full amount of time. You can also repackage and refreeze the food.

TIP 98: *Know the acidity of your vinegar*

🍯 Vinegar is not just for flavoring in a recipe. The acidity is an important component to safe preserving because it raises the acidity level of the food. But vinegar acidity can vary depending on the type. Check the acidity level on the label to ensure it is at least 5 percent acidity. Anything less and you could compromise the safety of your final product. Avoid using homemade vinegars or any vinegar with unknown acidity.

TIP 99: *Skip the hot-water bath or pressure canning*

🍯 The purpose of processing jars in a hot-water bath or pressure canner is to make them safe for long-term shelf storage. If you plan to use your canned foods within a few days or if you just run out of time, you can simply put them in the refrigerator. Most foods can be frozen in freezer containers for longer-term storage without processing.

TIP 100: *Bundle up herbs and spices for easy removal*

🍯 Some recipes call for herbs and spices to be added to food while it's cooking and then removed after. It can be tiresome to fish out all the disintegrated pieces of basil or tiny cloves from a sauce. Instead of tossing them right into the food, secure herbs and spices in small muslin bags that can be purchased at cooking supply stores. Or craft your own using cheesecloth and kitchen twine.

JAMS, JELLIES, AND SPREADS

TIP 101: *There is a difference between a jelly, jam, marmalade, and fruit butter*

Jellies, jams, marmalades, and fruit butters are all soft spreads. Jellies are made from strained or filtered juice. They do not contain any of the fruit peels or pulps, so they should be translucent. Jams are made from crushed or chopped fruits and are thick and spreadable. A marmalade is a jelly–jam hybrid. It contains pieces of fruit and fruit peels suspended in a translucent jelly. Butters are smooth spreads made from puréed fruit pulp. Unlike jellies, jams, and marmalades, butters should not be firm but rather like dairy butter—smooth, soft, and spreadable.

You may also hear people refer to preserves. It is a fuzzy term without a precise meaning that everyone agrees on. Used broadly, the term "preserve" means any food that has been processed for preserving. Preserve also refers to a fruit spread that incorporates pieces of whole or largely intact fruit in a jelly or syrup.

TIP 102: *Recognize what makes a quality jelly*

A quality jelly is clear or translucent because the fruit pulp is strained out using a jelly bag—so don't rush this part of the jelly-making process by squeezing or tapping the bag. Your jelly should be a bright color and firm enough to cut cleanly with a knife and still hold its shape. Still, it should be delicate enough to spread easily.

TIP 103: *Know what makes a quality jam and marmalade*

🍯 Jams and marmalades are made from whole fruit that has been cut into pieces or crushed. Marmalade also includes bits of the fruit peel or zest. Quality jams and marmalades should spread easily. They should be firm enough to create a mound on the spoon and have an even consistency with no excess liquid, but without being dry. Some people associate marmalade with a bitter flavor and tough fruit peels. Quality marmalades are never bitter and the peel is always soft.

TIP 104: *Fruit butters should be smooth*

🍯 Fruit butters are made with puréed fruit and sugar. They should be velvety smooth without any signs of fruit chunks or runny juices. To get this consistency, you'll need to use a food processor, immersion blender, or food mill rather than working manually. We all know about apple butter, but why stop there? You can make fruit butters from apricots, mangoes, bananas, peaches, pears—the list goes on!

TIP 105: *You can make jam the slow way or the fast way*

🍯 Traditional jams are made through long cooking and stirring. During the cooking process the fruit volume is decreased and flavors become more complex and concentrated. Additional pectin isn't necessary and fruit float is less likely. If you make jam this slow way, it helps to have a good-quality jam pot to help prevent sticking and scorching.

Quick-cook jams use pectin to help them achieve gel. Some people prefer the bright notes of the fresh fruit that come through in quick-cook jams. Fruit float is more likely with quick jams than with slow-cook jams, but that doesn't affect edibility; just stir the fruit back into the finished jam before serving.

TIP 106: *Pick a heavy jam pot*

The combination of heat and sugar makes jam easy to burn. To reduce the risk of ruining jam, pick a heavy-bottomed pot for the job. The best jam pot is made of lined copper and is low and wide with sloping sides. Unfortunately, it comes with a price tag that boggles the mind. You don't need to spend a fortune, though, if you pick a jam pot with the heaviest bottom you can find.

TIP 107: *Pick non-reactive pots for cooking high-acid foods*

Naturally occurring acids in some foods can react when cooked in aluminum, untreated cast iron, or unlined copper, leaching a metallic flavor into foods and causing discoloration. Always use a non-reactive pot made of stainless steel, enamel-lined cast iron, or lined copper when cooking such foods as strawberries, blueberries, and cranberries.

TIP 108: *Beware of doubling your fruit jam or jelly recipe*

Jam and jelly making are cases where more is not better. Making a double or triple batch at one time will require longer cooking time, which can cause the fruit to overcook and break up. It's better to make two separate batches.

TIP 109: *Take steps to prevent discoloration*

🔴 Some foods, such as apples and peaches, will discolor once they are peeled and exposed to air. Prevent browning by sprinkling produce with a commercial ascorbic acid mix available in stores that sell canning supplies. Or make your own solution by mixing ¾ cup lemon juice and a gallon (3.8L) of water. Submerge fruit until ready for use and drain well before cooking and canning.

TIP 110: *Try using frozen fruits for jam making*

🔴 Some fresh fruits, such as wild blueberries, may not be available where you live or when you want them. Other times fruits you wish to use may be of inferior quality. There may also be seasons when you are slammed with a bounty of produce that you don't have time to process into jams but do have time to freeze. In all of those cases, you can substitute frozen fruits and have excellent results in jam making. Fruits for jam making should be frozen without added sugar. Thaw fruits for jam and jelly making in the refrigerator until nearly all ice crystals have melted.

TIP 111: *Make jams and jellies on a dry day*

🔴 Some home preservers will warn you against making jams or jellies on a rainy day. The reasoning is that the jam or jelly will absorb moisture from the air, making it less likely that they will set properly. For most of us, this is probably less of an issue today than it was in the days before air conditioning made our lives so much more comfortable. If you find your rainy day jam or jelly didn't set and all the other factors that go into a successful jam or jelly were A-Okay, then try again—on a sunny day.

TIP 112: *Pectin firms jelly, jam, or marmalade to make it spreadable*

● Pectin is the natural thickening and gelling agent that makes jams, jellies, and other preserves spreadable rather than liquid and runny. The ratio of naturally occurring pectin in the fruit, additional pectin (if any), sugar, and acid determines how well the preserve gels and also the consistency of that gel. Fruit that is high in pectin may need no additional pectin to set. Lower-pectin produce can be combined with high-pectin fruits or may need added pectin in order to gel.

Pectin is available in almost any grocery or discount department store home goods section, although you may need to hunt around or ask for help finding it. Pectin and other canning supplies are often tucked away in completely illogical locations.

TIP 113: *Different fruits have different levels of pectin*

● Pectin levels vary between different types of fruit and even between more immature and fully ripe fruits of the same type. Pectin is more highly concentrated in underripe fruit and in seeds, pits, cores, rinds, and membranes of the fruit. High-pectin fruits include apples, citrus rinds, cranberries, currants, plums, grapes, and quinces. Low-pectin fruits include apricots, blueberries, cherries, peaches, pears, pineapples, raspberries, and strawberries. Vegetables, such as carrots, that are used in making jams and jellies are low in pectin.

TIP 114: *Experiment with different pectin formulations*

⊛ Commercially prepared pectins are available as liquids and powders and in sugar, low-sugar, no-sugar, and "premium" formulations. One popular brand of pectin contains a separate packet of calcium in the box, which makes it possible to use little or no sugar. To make matters even more confusing, package sizes vary, although you will find recipes that call for "one package of pectin" without giving you a clue about whether that is liquid or powder pectin or even a 1oz (28g) or 3oz (85g) package!

You will find home preservers who swear by one or the other pectin type. One camp swears that liquid pectins are more consistent, provide a more delicate set, and make a clearer jelly. The other camp proclaims that powdered pectins are more economical, particularly when purchased in bulk containers, are completely reliable, and can be stored longer than liquid pectins. A third camp wouldn't dream of using anything but homemade pectin. (More on that later.)

The bottom line is that liquid and powder pectins are not the same and are not interchangeable. You may wish to experiment and decide for yourself which you prefer. Either way, follow the recipe instructions carefully. If your recipe ingredient instructions regarding pectin are vague, find a similar, more precise recipe. You can also find simple pectin calculators on the Internet, although they are brand-specific.

TIP 115: *Make your own pectin*

You can make your own pectin—also called pectin stock—using tart apples, water, and lemon juice. Although some home preservers prefer to make their own pectin so they know where all their food is sourced, it adds time to the canning process and introduces an element of uncertainty.

Although all apples contain pectin, the amount varies depending on the maturity and variety of the apples and how highly you concentrate your final pectin stock. If you choose to go down the homemade pectin road, be prepared to test your products carefully for gel. Even then there could be some disappointments if your jam or jelly doesn't set.

There are many recipes and variations for making homemade pectin, but all involve using tart apples, water, and usually lemon juice boiled and strained to create the stock. Homemade pectin is perishable and must be used within a few days. You can also freeze homemade pectin, although that may affect its ability to gel. You will need to experiment with the amount of homemade pectin to use in your jams and jellies, but if you are a dedicated home preserver, you will be rewarded with an excellent product that is all your own.

TIP 116: *Buy pectin in bulk*

⚫ Pectin you can buy in grocery stores is sold in individual packets for use in a single batch. If you're going into jam, jelly, and other spread making in a big way, you can save money by buying pectin in bulk online. Bulk pectin is available in 1lb (450g), 10lb (4.5kg), and even 50lb (22.5kg) sizes. Most companies recommend that pectin be used within the year, but the pectin container should have an expiration date. Pectin that is older than a year isn't unsafe—just be aware that it may not work as well as fresh pectin.

TIP 117: *Avoid raw or crystallized sugar when making jams and jellies*

⚫ Sugar enhances the flavors of jams and jellies, assists in the preserving process, and helps to extract the juices from fruits. Some cooks prefer granulated cane sugar, and granulated beet sugar is also a good choice. Both cane and beet sugars are sold as white sugar in grocery stores; read the fine print to find out the sugar source. Avoid raw or crystallized sugar since the crystals are larger and may not dissolve well in the preserve.

TIP 118: *Make your own superfine sugar*

⚫ Foods, such as curds, that are not heated to the kind of high temperatures that break down sugar crystals sometimes call for superfine sugar. Superfine sugar, sometimes called caster sugar, is granulated sugar that has been ground into finer crystals than regular granulated white sugar. Superfine sugar can be difficult to find. Don't make the mistake of thinking confectioners' sugar is superfine sugar. It's not. If you can't find superfine sugar, you can substitute granulated white sugar processed briefly in a blender or food processor.

TIP 119: *Try substituting honey or agave for sugar in a recipe*

You can substitute sugar with honey or agave, but there are some differences you should consider first. Honey and agave are actually sweeter than sugar. A cup-for-cup substitution could leave you with a jam or jelly that is much sweeter than you intended. Second, different honeys and agaves have different flavors. Some honeys, such as the widely available clover honey you can easily find in grocery stores, are mild and fairly light. Other honeys, such as heather honey, have a pungent, almost bitter flavor.

If you're just starting to experiment with honey or agave as a sweetening substitute, try substituting just part of the sugar in the recipe. For example, you could use 1/2 cup of honey or agave and a cup of sugar in a recipe that calls for 2 cups of sugar.

TIP 120: *Macerate your fruit*

Sugar does wonderful things when allowed to visit with fruit for a few hours, which is really all maceration is. Sugar draws the fruit juices out of the fruit to create a wonderfully flavored syrup. In addition, the texture of some tough-textured fruits, such as rhubarb, is improved through maceration. To macerate fruit, sprinkle it with sugar, stir well so the sugar covers the fruit, and allow it to sit for several hours or overnight before proceeding with your recipe.

TIP 121: *Use a potato masher to crush fruit during jam making*

🥄 You can use a wooden spoon on the side of the jam pot to crush a portion of the cherries, strawberries, or other fruit for jam. A less time-consuming method is to use a potato masher. Just give the fruit a few mashes to crush a portion of the berries. It will help to extract the juices and provide a nice consistency to the jam.

TIP 122: *Soften citrus peels with baking soda*

🥄 Grapefruit, orange, and lemon peels used in marmalades should be tender, never tough. Peels should be stripped from the fruit to avoid the white, bitter pith. Before using in your recipe, tenderize the peels by simmering them for 20 minutes with $1/8$ tsp of baking soda in $2^1/2$ cups (600ml) of water.

TIP 123: *Sugar substitutes can be used for some, but not all, canned foods*

🥄 Sugar is essential in some recipes because it has important preserving properties for canned foods that will be stored at room temperature. Nevertheless, the sugar substitute Splenda® (sucralose) can be used when canning fruits that can be canned in plain water. You won't get the same thick syrup you would get using sugar and you may notice some aftertaste. In recipes where sugar is an important preservative, as in some preserves and pickled fruits, sugar substitutes are not recommended. You can use Splenda as a sweetener in sugarless fruit spread recipes that are made with special no-sugar-needed pectins. Read labels and instructions carefully for how to use sugar substitutes.

TIP 124: Don't skip the acid

⚫ Acids are sometimes used to bring out the flavors in recipes and improve consistency. Acids such as lemon juice and vinegar also help to raise the acid level—an important element in inhibiting bacteria growth for safe preserving. Don't skip or reduce this important recipe ingredient.

TIP 125: Look into electric jam makers

⚫ Electric jam makers work similarly to slow cookers—pour in the ingredients, plug it in, and the appliance does the work. Jam makers have stirring mechanisms that keep the jelly or jam moving during the cooking process. An electric jam maker could be a nice investment if you love homemade slow-cooked jam but have physical difficulty standing for long periods at the stove. It also could be a real boon for parents of busy children who worry about scalding jelly on a hot stove or constantly being interrupted by a jam-making process that can take several minutes.

TIP 126: Try a microwave jam recipe

⚫ If you don't have time for a full-blown jam making and processing project, you can make a quickie jam by using a recipe that takes advantage of your microwave oven. You can make two to four ½-pint (250ml) jars of jam in about 30 minutes of hands-on work time. Since it isn't processed in a hot-water bath canner, microwave jams should be eaten right away or stored in the refrigerator.

TIP 127: Take extra safety steps when making jams, jellies, and other spreads

⬤ With big pots of boiling water, it's obvious that safety precautions are a priority for any canning project. This is particularly true when making jams, jellies, and other spreads since boiling fruit and sugar is extremely hot and can bubble and spatter. It's a good idea to wear long sleeves to protect your arms from unexpected drips and splashes. Before cooking your spreads, set aside a bowl of ice water to use for emergencies. If you are burned, immerse the affected area in the water as quickly as possible.

TIP 128: Test for gel using the plate or spoon method

⬤ Before cooking your jam or jelly, place a few small plates in the refrigerator or freezer that you will use to test the gel, or set, of your preserves. When you are ready to test, pour a small amount of the jam or jelly onto the plate and return it to the refrigerator for 5 minutes. To test, use your finger to gently push the edge of the mixture. If it wrinkles, it is ready. If not, continue cooking and try again in a couple of minutes on another cold plate.

Alternatively, you can use a metal spoon that you have refrigerated. Dip the spoon into the boiling jelly or jam mixture and watch how the mixture sheets off the spoon as you hold it on its side so the syrup can run off. When you begin cooking, the drops will be quite liquid. As the syrup is nearly done, the drops will become thicker and drop off the spoon more slowly. When two drops form together and "sheet" off the spoon, the gel point has been reached.

TIP 129: Use a candy thermometer to test for gel

If using a chilled plate or spoon to test the gel of a jelly or jam is too subjective for your taste, you can use a candy thermometer. Place the candy thermometer in the jam or jelly but don't set it directly on the bottom of the jam pot that is in contact with the heating element. You want to test the temperature of the food, not the pot. Read the thermometer at eye level for accuracy. The jelly or jam is done when the temperature reaches 220°F (105°C).

TIP 130: Beware of overcooking

Resist the urge to keep cooking to ensure that your jam or jelly will set. Overcooking can damage the flavor of your preserves.

TIP 131: Set aside plenty of time to make jelly

Great jellies take time. In fact, some home preservers consider jelly making a 2-day process. On the first day, the juice is extracted from the fruit and then filtered so that it is clear. The juice is then allowed to rest overnight in the refrigerator so that any remaining sediment will settle to the bottom. On the second day, the juice is filtered again and then mixed with sugar, cooked, and processed. Attempts to speed up the process can result in a cloudy jelly that is edible, but certainly less appealing. So just plan for a lengthy process.

TIP 132: *Try using a sieve and cheesecloth to make clear jellies*

⚫ Specialized jelly bags with metal frames to attach to bowls are available at hardware stores and other places where canning supplies are sold. The problem is that some jelly bags are made of such a tight weave that the fruit clogs the fabric. You have to keep disassembling the bag and cleaning it. Sometimes bits of pulp end up in the juice. Frankly, it can be frustrating. It's understandable that some home preservers resort to squeezing the bag to extract the juice. Unfortunately, this is a mistake, because it allows small pieces of the fruit to slip through, resulting in a cloudy jelly.

Try using a sieve and cheesecloth instead. Depending on the density of the cheesecloth weave, you will need to double or triple fold the fabric. Also, dampen it first to keep the cheesecloth from absorbing too much of the precious juice. You may need to strain your jelly two or three times.

TIP 133: *Skim the foam*

⚫ Don't be alarmed if your jam or jelly foams while cooking. Simply skim off the foam with a spoon. Although some cooks stir in a small pat of butter at the end of cooking to disperse any remaining foam, this practice isn't recommended since fats don't preserve well and could promote spoilage.

TIP 134: *Use a wooden or plastic spoon to stir jams, jellies, and other spreads*

⚫ Using a whisk introduces air bubbles that you'll need to take pains to remove before processing. Aluminum spoons can react with the food, causing discoloration. Use a wooden or plastic spoon instead when making jams, jellies, and spreads.

TIP 135: *Avoid making cloudy jellies*

🍓 The best jellies should be shimmering and clear or translucent. If your homemade jelly looks cloudy or murky, review your preparation methods. Don't use underripe fruits, which may have starches that will cloud jellies. Proper fruit preparation and cooking are extremely important. Foams produced in the cooking process should be meticulously skimmed off. Don't squeeze the jelly bag or cheesecloth during juice extraction or you risk getting tiny parts of the fruit in the juice, which can cloud your jelly. Finally, work quickly after cooking. Don't allow your cooked jelly mixture to cool before filling jars and processing.

TIP 136: *Make refrigerator or freezer jam*

🍓 If you don't have enough time or energy for a full-blown canning project, have excess freezer space, or just can't face having a cauldron of water boiling in your kitchen on a hot summer day, you can make refrigerator or freezer jam. Use fresh or frozen uncooked fruit. Chop or crush the fruit and mix it with sugar, fruit juice, and pectin according to the directions on your pectin container. Pack into clean, sterilized freezer containers, allowing 1in (2.5cm) of headspace for expansion during freezing. Let stand at room temperature for 24 hours before freezing to allow for the sugar, fruit, and juices to combine. No-cook jams will keep in the refrigerator for 3 weeks or up to a year in the freezer. Once opened, they should be refrigerated and used within a few days.

TIP 137: *Give foods containing spices and herbs time*

🍯 Foods containing cinnamon, cloves, dill, and other spices and herbs take time to fully develop. You can open and eat the foods right away, but the flavors will be more complex and delicious if you wait 2–3 weeks before digging in.

TIP 138: *Know that your yield will vary*

🍯 The number of jars you get from a given amount of produce is likely to vary. This is because the water content varies from one batch of fruit to another. The amount of sugar you use and how much you reduce your spread mixture in the cooking process will all be factors. Over time you'll learn to estimate your yield, but it will never be an exact science.

TIP 139: *Don't throw away runny jellies and jams*

🍯 It is disappointing when your strawberry jam or grape jelly drips off the spoon like syrup. Jams and jellies achieve that marvelous gel when there is the right ratio of acid, pectin, and sugar, so avoid adjusting recipes or you risk altering the balance that will make the difference between success and failure. Old pectin or an insufficient amount of pectin, not enough acid, overripe fruit, doubling a recipe, and cooking too much or cooking too little or for too long are all reasons a spread can fail to set. Know too that homemade pectins can vary widely in concentration.

If your jam or jelly doesn't set in the proper time, don't throw it away. You can reprocess the spread by reheating, adjusting the sugar, acid, or pectin level, recooking and reprocessing. Of course, there is no guarantee that your jam or jelly will set through reprocessing, so you might want to rename it "syrup" and use it as a topping on waffles, pancakes, and ice cream.

FRUITS AND VEGETABLES

TIP 140: *Have two types of vegetable peelers*

🥫 The vegetable peeler may be the most underutilized gadget in the kitchen. It isn't uncommon for vegetables such as potatoes, carrots, and—heaven forbid—cucumbers to be peeled with a paring knife, leaving all sorts of good vegetable to go down the disposal. You should consider having at least two types of vegetable peelers among your kitchen equipment. A swivel peeler is a good all-purpose peeler that allows you to easily maneuver around the contours of produce to remove peels and skins without sacrificing an excessive amount of the fruit or vegetable. A Y-shaped vegetable peeler offers more control when peeling large and tough fruits and vegetables. They are strong enough to peel even a winter squash. Some Y-shaped peelers have a julienne blade for making quick work of slicing matchstick carrots and other vegetables.

TIP 141: *Invest in a Microplane® for grating*

🥫 There are small zesting tools available that work fine for small amounts of lemon or lime zest you may need in your recipe. If you're going to be using lots of zest or doing other fine grating for your recipes, add a Microplane to your kitchen arsenal. A Microplane looks like a long, narrow, fine grater because that is, in fact, what it is. It is perfect for grating foods such as chocolate, hard cheese, citrus zest, coconut, ginger, and garlic.

TIP 142: *Learn how to pit stone fruits quickly*

If your project involves canning peaches or other stone fruits—fruits with one big seed in the center—make short work of preparation. Make a cut around the circumference of the fruit horizontally, so you're slicing from the stem to the bottom all the way around on both sides. Slightly twist the two halves of the fruit in opposite directions. You should be able to gently ease the two sides apart. Use a spoon to scoop out the pit.

TIP 143: *How to peel that pesky peach*

Peaches are wonderful for canning, but peeling them can be a frustrating experience. Here is a way to help you overcome the peach that refuses to be peeled. Fill a 3-quart (2.8L) saucepan with 2½ quarts (2.4L) of water and bring to a boil. Fill a separate bowl with water and add ice cubes. Using a paring knife, make an X opposite the stem end of each peach. Drop the peaches into boiling water and then count to 14 and remove the peaches from the boiling water with a slotted spoon to the iced water. Finally, use your fingers to remove the skin from the peaches after they are cooled. The end result should be a more smooth and shapely peach that is free of the frustrating angles and gouges that result from more conventional methods of peeling.

TIP 144: *Know how to ripen fruit more quickly*

If you have underripe fruit and want to expedite the ripening in preparation for canning, you can do so by placing the fruit in a loosely closed paper bag. This in turn will trap some of the ethylene gas that is released by the fruit and accelerate the ripening process. One modification of this process is to place an apple in the bag as well, which may expedite the process. Leave it overnight and check it in the morning to see how your fruit is doing.

TIP 145: *Pick the right apple for the job*

There are about 7,500 known cultivars of apples, with different colors, sizes, textures, degrees of sweetness, and other qualities. The apple producers' industry has gone to extraordinary lengths to test the various uses of the different apple types to match them for specific culinary uses.

For best results for a canning project, pick the right apple for your intended use. In general, sweeter and softer apples, such as Gala and Fuji apples, make the best applesauce. Firmer apples with less moisture content, such as Rome apples, are often preferred for baking and storing. Crisp and juicy apples, such as Honeycrisps, are excellent for just eating right out of your hand. Grocery store signage often has recommended uses for the apple types on display. Familiarize yourself with the various apple characteristics so the next time you're ready for an apple-canning project, you know which variety of apple to reach for.

TIP 146: *Use berries and figs quickly or they will mold*

🍓 Figs, blueberries, strawberries, and other berries and high-moisture fruits will go from sublime to moldy in no time. Plan to can these fruits as quickly as possible after you bring them home. Pick through the berries carefully, discarding any that are bruised, overripe, or otherwise damaged. Fresh figs can be spoiled and still look fine on the outside. Slice through the center of some samples to check for quality to avoid canning spoiled fruit.

TIP 147: *Use specialized tools to speed up produce prep work*

🍓 There is a wide range of specialized kitchen gadgets that can make peeling, pitting, and other produce prep work a snap. You may not need them all or even need them very often, but they can make a real difference in your workflow and even in the appearance of your final product. Browse online or in kitchen specialty shops for cherry pitters, apple and pineapple corers, apple peelers, and other useful and time-saving kitchen gadgets.

TIP 148: *Uniform is best when it comes to slicing and dicing fruits and vegetables*

🍓 Take the time to carefully slice and dice bits of fruit and vegetables so they are as close to the same size and shape as possible. It's not just a matter of aesthetics, although it is certainly more attractive. Uniform sizes cook more evenly, contributing to a better-quality product.

TIP 149: Blanch fruits and vegetables for easy peeling

To make peeling tomatoes, pearl onions, and even citrus fruits a snap, blanch them quickly before peeling. Blanch thin-skinned produce, such as tomatoes, for about 10 seconds and then plunge into cold water. The skins will slide right off. Thicker-skinned produce, such as lemons, will take longer—up to a minute—but will peel more easily.

TIP 150: Think strategically about packing jars

Many fruits and vegetables will shrink during processing and storage, leaving them floating in water or syrup. Think strategically about how to get as many pieces of produce into a jar to minimize floaters. Okra, for example, shrinks considerably. Pack whole okra in layers, with one layer tips down and one layer tips up nestled between the lower layers.

TIP 151: Knowing in advance the ratio of fruit to jars can help limit expense and waste

It is helpful to know in advance about how much fruit you will need per jar. For example, for whole cherries an average of $17\frac{1}{2}$lb (8kg) is needed per canner load of 7 quarts (6.6L). Or with berries as another example, an average of 12lb (5.5kg) is needed per canner load of 7 quarts while an average of 8lb (3.6kg) is needed per canner load of 9 pints (4.25L). It's not exact. Yield estimates are just that—estimates. But knowing this information in advance will help you better plan for how many jars you may need while mitigating waste.

TIP 152: *Don't waste trimmings and rinds*

🍓 Some produce, such as carrots or asparagus, will need to be trimmed to fit vertically into a jar. It would be a shame and a waste to throw away those tender ends. Instead, use them in soups or lightly steam them to include in salads. Save watermelon rinds for pickling. If you can't think of any other use for fruit cores and peelings, feed them to the birds!

TIP 153: *Don't alter the recipe by adding extra low-acid foods*

🍓 You may love onions, celery, or sweet peppers, but don't be tempted to toss in an extra handful beyond what the recipe calls for. Such foods are low-acid foods. Altering the ratio of foods in a recipe can make the pH less acid, an important factor in determining safe processing methods and time. If you really want extra onions, find another recipe.

TIP 154: *Use ClearJel® when canning fruit pie fillings*

🍓 The USDA's National Center for Food Preservation recommends using ClearJel to thicken fruit pie fillings for canning. Cornstarch, flour, and other fillings can break down and give a filling a runny consistency. ClearJel is a modified cornstarch that helps to give the sauce in the filling an even consistency.

TIP 155: *Do not add butter, bacon, or other fatty ingredients*

⬤ Butter, bacon, or other fatty ingredients should not be added to a recipe unless it is specified. Fats do not store well and will contribute to the deterioration and spoilage of any canned product. Some home preservers will tell you to add a pat of butter to reduce the foaming of jams and jellies. This really isn't necessary if you just skim it off.

TIP 156: *You have many choices when it comes to packing fruits*

⬤ Fruits can be packed in water and in extra-light, light, medium, heavy, or extra-heavy syrups. What choices! Syrups are made with sugar, honey, or corn syrup mixed with water and then cooked to a boil. Sweetened syrups help keep the shape, color, and firmness of a fruit in storage. Fruits canned in a heavy syrup are more likely to float, especially if they are raw-packed. Don't worry though. It's just an aesthetic problem and the fruit is still perfectly safe.

TIP 157: *Use up all that fruit syrup*

⬤ The syrup used to pack fruits is wonderfully flavorful all by itself. If you have used all the fruit and still have syrup left, use it to pour over ice cream, flavor tea, or moisten pound cake. You could also just drink it up!

PICKLES, RELISHES, AND CHUTNEYS

TIP 158: *Pick the right bowls and pots for pickling*

Avoid containers and utensils made of unlined copper, iron, zinc, or brass when pickling. These materials may react with acid and salt and can cloud or discolor your pickles. For pots, pick such materials as stainless steel, heatproof glass, or hard-anodized aluminum.

TIP 159: *Put your leftover brine to good use*

If you have leftover brine, don't just pour it down the drain! Make some quick-pickled onions. Just thin-slice onions and cover with brine and refrigerate to marinate. They are delicious on sandwiches, salads, or tossed into roasted vegetable dishes.

TIP 160: *Take steps to make crisp pickles*

Wonderfully crisp cucumbers must be made with the right pickles. Pickling cucumbers are smaller, have fewer seeds and less-bitter skin than salad cucumbers. The Burpless and English cucumbers commonly used in salads are not good choices if you want quality, crisp pickles. Good varieties for pickling include Eureka, Carolina, and West India Gherkin. Choose cucumbers that are ripe, but not overripe. The fresher the cucumber, the better will be your result. Take time to trim off the blossom end of the cucumber, which could contain enzymes that can cause softening. Finally, don't overprocess jars and carefully follow the recipe instructions regarding the ratio of vinegar to water, since too much vinegar can make for mushy pickles.

TIP 161: *Understand the causes of pickle problems*

⬤ Almost all pickle problems can be traced back to a specific cause. Pickles that are soft or slippery could be caused by a problem with the brine—either the vinegar was not at least 5 percent acidity or there was an insufficient amount of brine. Pickles that were improperly processed or blossom ends left on the cucumber could also cause this problem. Shriveled pickles can also be caused by a problem with the brine being either too strong, too heavy on the syrup, or having a too-strong vinegar. Spotted, dull, or faded-looking pickles could have been exposed to too much light. The cucumbers could also have been of poor quality. The bottom line is that if something is not quite right with your pickles, think through your ingredients and process.

TIP 162: *Know how to fix too-tart pickles*

⬤ The perfect pickle can be picky. Occasionally you may use a recipe that produced a pucker-producing pickle. If the recipe is a family hand-me-down or otherwise appeals to you and you want to use it again, don't reduce the amount of vinegar in search of the too-tart cure. The vinegar is an important safety ingredient to prevent the growth of bacteria. Instead, add a bit of sugar to the mix.

TIP 163: *Use the right kind of salt*

🖤 Canning recipes usually specify that you use pickling salt, canning salt, or preserving salt. They're all the same thing and are really just fine-grained, pure salt without the anti-caking or iodine additives typically found in table salt. You want to avoid these additives; although they won't hurt you, they can turn preserved foods dark and cloud liquids or leave a white sediment in the jar. Don't assume that because you use kosher salt it doesn't have additives, because some do. Read labels carefully and pick a salt without additives.

You should also know that coarser salts take longer to dissolve, which can be an important consideration in cold-packed foods. If you are substituting another salt for pickling salt, you will also need to adjust the measurements since other salts will have larger grains and not pack as tightly together in the measuring spoon. A teaspoon of pickling salt is about equal to $1\frac{1}{4}$tsp of kosher salt. There are more extensive salt conversion charts on the Internet.

TIP 164: *Make your own pickling spices*

🖤 Customize your homemade pickles with your own brand of pickling spices. Experiment with specialized combinations of crushed and crumbled spices and herbs such as coriander, fennel, caraway and mustard seeds, peppercorns, dried pepper flakes, allspice, bay leaves, ginger, chilies, and cloves. Mix spices in small batches for optimal freshness. Briefly toast pickling spices in a dry sauté pan to bring out flavors immediately before using in recipes.

TIP 165: *Use fresh dill when making dill pickles*

⚙ Dill is such an important ingredient in dill pickles that you should use fresh, not dried. In fact, the fresher the dill the better. Use a whole dill head for each jar, cutting it into florets and packing at the bottom and even adding a bit more on the top, if you wish.

TIP 166: *Make pickles in the freezer*

⚙ This sounds very counter-intuitive since everyone knows cucumbers don't freeze well. But this works to make wonderful pickles! Wash and thinly slice 4 cups of good pickling cucumbers and two large onions. Mix together with 1 tbsp of salt and let stand for 2–4 hours at room temperature to extract the moisture from the vegetables. Rinse, drain, and blot well with paper towels. In a separate bowl, combine 1 cup of sugar, $\frac{1}{2}$ cup of cider vinegar, 1 tbsp of white mustard seeds, and $\frac{1}{2}$ tsp of turmeric and mix until all the ingredients are dissolved. Pour the liquid over the cucumber and onions, pack into freezer containers, and seal. When you're ready to eat, just thaw in the refrigerator for a few hours and eat!

TIP 167: *Wait a while before opening your pickles—or not*

⚫ Many pickle recipes will indicate how long you should wait before opening the jar and eating. Refrigerator pickles are usually ready in a few days. Cold-pack or other non-fermented pickles can take as little as a week or as long as 3 months until the flavors are fully developed.

In general, there are two schools of thought about how long to wait until you open and eat your pickles. The first school says if you have gone to the trouble of slicing, brining, and processing, why not wait a few weeks so they are at their peak. The second school of thought says, if they taste good to you and you want to eat them, then go ahead. The fact is, unless you eat all the jars of pickles at one time, you can have it both ways! Eat a jar pretty much right away. Eat another jar next week. Another jar after that. You'll figure out for yourself how long is best to wait by sampling.

TIP 168: *Try pickled eggs*

⚫ If you traveled through Britain years ago you may have seen jars of pickled eggs on the counters in pub bars. In the Pennsylvania Dutch country there is a popular version of beet-pickled eggs that are an attractive pink. Pickled eggs can be spicy too, such as those made with hot sauce.

You can pickle any sort of eggs, but the best eggs for pickling are small ones. Small chicken eggs are fine. Pheasant, guinea, and quail eggs are delightful. Duck and goose eggs are larger and less suitable for pickling.

Unfortunately, there are no safe methods for canning pickled eggs at home. But you don't have to bypass this old-fashioned treat. You can still pickle eggs and keep them in the refrigerator—they should be used within 3–4 months for best quality. Never leave pickled eggs at room temperature except when serving.

TIP 169: *Discover the vast array of relish possibilities*

⚫ Given how much most people enjoy eating, it's remarkable how few of us seem to relish relishes. For most people, relish is limited to those confetti-sized sweet bits you put on a hot dog. There is so much more to relishes than that. In general, a relish is a sweet, savory, and/or sour sauce mixed with a chopped and pickled vegetable or mix of vegetables, but also sometimes fruits. Many, but not all, relishes are developed specifically to complement foods, as a kind of exclamation point to the side or on top—or underneath. But some relishes are more than just condiments. Some are meant to be eaten all by themselves.

The very definition gives quite a lot of leeway as to what goes into a relish, since what seems to hold the whole idea together are the words "sauce" and "chopped." Browse through the grocery store condiment aisle, though, and you're likely to find very few relishes, largely confined to pickled cucumber and pepper relishes. You may find some version of a corn relish, but you would do better to make your own with crisp, sweet summer corn so you can sneak in some colorful carrots and jalapenos. How about a fennel relish so you can stretch that delightful, but underused, vegetable onto plates with blackened salmon or spicy pork chops? We like olive and caper relishes, also called tapenades, and the unusual relishes you can eat as salads made from green beans, beets, or rhubarb.

TIP 170: *Use a food processor, food mill, or meat grinder to get the best relish consistency*

● The most tedious and time-consuming task of relish making is chopping the produce into quite small and uniform pieces so that it can soak up and blend into the relish sauce. This is the time to pull the food processor or other mechanical kitchen device from under the counter and put it to work.

Food processors fitted with a metal chopping blade will make short work of vegetables. In fact, if you are making a lemon–zucchini relish, for example, you'll likely cut your vegetable preparation time down from 30 minutes to 30 seconds. But the pieces may be less uniform than you like, although you can improve on the results by using short on and off bursts of power rather than just turning the processor on and letting it run. Food mills with disks that can be switched out for different consistencies are a good choice as are food grinders, also called meat grinders, with different plate sizes.

TIP 171: *Seed cucumbers for use in relishes*

● In bread and butter pickle or dill pickle making, you leave the few cucumber seeds in place, since they are an integral part of the dish. Cucumber seeds and pulp should be removed in making relish so the pulp doesn't dilute the sauce and the seeds don't interfere with the delicate consistency of the small bits of pickle.

Seeding cucumbers is quite easy and doesn't require any special tool. Before chopping, slice cucumbers lengthwise. Using a melon baller, spoon, or even your fingers, gently scoop out the seeds and pulp, taking care not to scrape away the meat of the cucumber.

TIP 172: *You can make no-sugar relishes at home*

Although the range of no-sugar alternatives is increasing, most store-bought relishes include copious amounts of sugar. This is yet another reason why canning is having a renewed surge in popularity. Many people have special dietary needs and preferences that are more easily met by avoiding commercially prepared foods and making foods at home.

There are many recipes for no-sugar relishes, including the traditional hot dog pickle relish. Some recipes use Splenda® as a sweetener and others mix in naturally sweet vegetables, such as carrots, to give the relish a sweeter flavor. Even if you choose to use no sweetening alternative, you may find that you prefer no-sugar relishes for their more piquant vegetable flavors unmasked by sweeteners.

TIP 173: *Try making chutneys that will add spice and flavor to meals*

There is some fuzzy overlap between the definition of chutneys and relishes. Like relishes, chutneys are made from fruits and vegetables, but more often fruits. Chutneys can be thick, somewhat like a marmalade, but can also be syrupy, like a relish. The consistency often includes larger chunks than relishes. Perhaps it is because of their origins and popularity in South Asian cuisine that chutneys are usually more highly spiced than relishes—although they don't have to be. Yes, it's quite a fuzzy business.

Combine your food drying and canning efforts by making a savory fruit chutney from dried peaches, plums, nectarines, red onions, and bell peppers along with coriander and mint. You could make a traditional cranberry chutney. Or visit an Indian grocery store and find some tamarind paste to make any number of traditional Indian chutneys.

TIP 174: *Make your own Major Grey's Mango Chutney*

Major Grey's Mango Chutney may be the only chutney most people in the Western world could name in a speed contest. That's because it is so popular here that it is almost the generic definition of chutney. Major Grey's isn't a brand of chutney because there are dozens of brands of Major Grey's Mango Chutney. Rather it is the type of chutney made with mangoes, raisins, and onions, along with vinegar and spices. The name supposedly comes from the 19th-century British Army officer who invented the stuff. Major Grey is probably mythical, or at least he is lost to time, but the chutney endures because it is so absolutely delicious.

The list of ingredients to make your own Major Grey's is quite long, so print out a recipe to take to the grocery store to find the spices you'll need or you'll surely forget something. You'll be happy to have several pints on hand not only to serve with meats, but to mix with grated cheese for sandwiches, to give a new twist to chicken salad, to top baked *brie en croûte* or to entice your children to eat their vegetables.

SOUPS AND SOUP STOCKS

TIP 175: *Plan to use a pressure canner to process soups*

There is no getting around the fact that soups must be processed in the pressure canner. The vegetables and meats are all below the safe acidity level for hot-water bath canning. If you don't have a pressure canner or don't want to use one, freeze your soups instead.

TIP 176: *Take the time to cut vegetables into small bites for chunky soups*

Think about how you eat soup. It's one spoonful at a time. If you're eating a vegetable soup, you probably don't want to eat a spoonful of a big green bean, a spoonful of a carrot chunk, and then a spoonful of half a tomato. You want a little bit of each when you put a spoonful in your mouth. Think about this when you are chopping vegetables for chunky soups and make the pieces small enough to fit a couple or three vegetables on the spoon at a time.

TIP 177: *Fill jars so the soup solids are evenly distributed*

When filling jars with soup, first use a slotted spoon to scoop out the soup's solid ingredients and distribute them evenly between all the number of jars you intend to fill. Once the solids have been filled, ladle in the broth. If you find that you have one jar only partially full, you can refrigerate it and eat it soon. Alternatively, you can spoon some of the broth out of the filled jars and spoon in some of the solids from the partially filled jar.

TIP 178: *Do not add noodles, other pasta, white rice, or thickeners to soups before processing*

🥣 Noodles, other pasta, and white rice become waterlogged and soggy when canned. Even if you don't mind soggy noodles, don't can these foods because they slow the penetration of heat through the jars in processing, leaving the soup underprocessed and unsafe to eat. Also, do not add any flour, cream, eggs, or milk as thickeners since they don't process well in the pressure canner. You can add all of these ingredients later, when you are heating to serve. Brown rice, wild rice, and other less-processed rice hold up better than white, converted, or instant rice.

TIP 179: *Cook all soup ingredients so they are ready for serving*

🥣 Don't plan to undercook vegetables—and certainly not meats—thinking that they will be cooked further when you heat the soup for serving. Dried beans used in soups must be completely rehydrated and cooked as well.

TIP 180: *Purée soups just prior to serving*

🥣 Puréeing vegetables increases the density of the produce in the jar and thus alters the acidity level. It is for this reason that it is not recommended that you purée soups prior to pressure-canner processing.

TIP 181: Stock up on stock

Having a ready supply of canned chicken, beef, or vegetable stock can be a convenience and a timesaver. Sure, you can freeze stock, but then you have to remember to thaw it. It also will take up valuable real estate in the freezer that you can use for other items.

The French call the vegetable triad of onions, celery, and carrots that make up the vegetable part of stock *mirepoix*. The Italians have a similar combination they call *soffrito*. Add to those beef, chicken, veal, or other cracked or crushed bones for maximum flavor. A thrifty way to make a meat stock is to save up meat bones you would otherwise throw away. Just keep them in the freezer until you have enough to make a batch of stock. Stock is a low-acid food and must be processed in a pressure canner.

TIP 182: Know the secret to making a savory vegetable broth

Store-bought vegetable broth is dreadful. This is definitely the broth you need to make at home. Feel free to use scraps and pieces of vegetables that you have squirreled away, but don't think that the vegetable broth is the place for every sad-looking vegetable that has been lingering for weeks in your vegetable bin. Use only the best scraps and be prepared to add some fresh onions, carrots, and celery to round out the spare mushroom stems, rutabagas, or other vegetables you have. Good choices include leeks, parsnips, fennel, and broccoli. To extract the best, most savory, flavors, roast the vegetables before turning them into stock.

TIP 183: Don't be afraid to use chicken skin and feet in making stock

⬤ Parts of the chicken you wouldn't ordinarily eat can make a significant flavor contribution to your stock. Chicken skin and feet, in particular, are loaded with collagen, which will improve the body and texture of your stock. Feel free to use the giblets that come in the little bag stuffed into the cavity of the chicken, but leave out the liver, which can cloud your broth.

TIP 184: Try making fish broth

⬤ A fish broth is delicate and delicious. You can use fish broths in seafood-based dishes, such as chowders, paella, and risottos, as well as for the base of a wonderful, homemade miso soup.

To make fish broth, use bones from lean, white fish, such as halibut or sole. Stock made from salmon and other oily fish bones will be overpowering. Round out the ingredients with onions, celery, and carrots, but consider adding mushrooms and herbs, such as thyme, dill, or tarragon.

TIP 185: Skim fat off of stock used for canning

⬤ The process of simmering bones to make stock inevitably produces fat that rises to the top during cooking. This fat should be regularly skimmed off during the simmering process. Extra fat that ends up in the canning jar makes for a poor product that can turn rancid and spoil.

It is nearly impossible to skim all the fat from stock. You can use a spoon to skim fat, but it can be tedious work. Fat separators and mesh skimmers are available, which will make the job easier. Since stock-making itself is a time-intensive project, you might consider straddling the whole job over 2 days. Make the stock on the first day and refrigerate it overnight. The next day, any remaining fats will have congealed at the top and can easily be skimmed off. Reheat the stock before straining and processing in a pressure canner.

TIP 186: Strain your broth before canning

⬤ A broth should be quite clear and free of any tiny bits of meat or vegetable. Meticulously strain broth before pouring into jars and processing. Use a fine sieve or a cheesecloth-lined colander and drain into a large bowl or pot. You may need to repeat the process a couple of times. If your broth tastes a bit watery and bland after straining, you can reduce it to concentrate the flavors before bottling and canning.

MEATS AND SEAFOOD

TIP 187: *You must use a pressure canner and use it properly when canning meats and seafood*

● There is no room for error when it comes to canning meats and seafood. The high protein content and fat make meats and seafood much more susceptible to contamination and spoilage than fruits and vegetables. Consider carefully if canning is your best option or if freezing is a better alternative for you. If you do can meats or seafood, make sure your pressure gauge is accurate. You may want to consider having your local agricultural extension agent or manufacturer check and calibrate your dial gauge. Read pressure canner instructions and follow them to the letter, making sure that you adjust processing times if you live at an altitude above 1,000ft (300m).

TIP 188: *Consider consulting the experts when canning meat or seafood*

● Canning meat and seafood can be a rewarding, nutritional, and indeed tasteful experience. The process, though, should be treated with caution and conducted carefully because even small errors can lead to a bad result. Therefore, before starting out, if you are a novice, consult the many readily available and free resources that are available from the USDA, state departments of agriculture, fisheries, or natural resources, and your state and local agricultural extension services. When it comes to canning meat or seafood, there is no such thing as being too careful or too well informed.

TIP 189: In canning, particularly with meat and seafood, use only quality canning equipment

⬤ Do not take shortcuts in canning when it comes to procuring equipment. This is particularly true with regard to canning meat and seafood. For example, use only standard glass mason-type jars and a two-piece flat lid and screw band. The bottom line is that any old jar from the basement, or any old pot for boiling water, for that matter, won't do. Use a proper pressure canner with a properly calibrated gauge.

TIP 190: Know how to evaluate the freshness of fish

⬤ Fish is probably one of the most difficult foods to buy. Not only is there less familiarity with a lot of the fish varieties, but fish is also highly perishable, can be farm or wild-raised, fresh, frozen, or thawed for sale. To make matters worse, many grocery stores sell fish in poor condition.

Choose a store that specializes in seafood and that has a high product turnover. Don't be afraid to ask to inspect and smell the fish, although don't expect to be able to hold it. A slight fishy smell is normal, but avoid any fish that smells strongly of fish. It is an early sign that the fish is past its prime. It helps to know the country of origin of the fish, particularly if it is farm-raised. Other countries may use drugs that are banned in the United States. Moreover, overseas fish farms are not inspected by U.S. officials and only a small fraction of imported seafood is tested for drug residues.

You can tell a lot by how a fish looks. Precut fish should look moist and shiny, without signs of drying or brown edges. Whole fish should have a glossy, taut-looking skin. Avoid fish with sunken, clouded eyes or brown gills. Some fish may have added colors, but should also be labeled as such.

TIP 191: Take a cooler with you when you buy fish

🐟 If you know your errands include buying fish for dinner or for a canning project, put a cooler with ice in the car to take with you. Fish begin to deteriorate as soon as they die and even a small time at a higher temperature can hasten the decline. If you forget, ask the fishmonger to provide you with a bit of bagged ice to help keep your fish chilled.

TIP 192: Consider buying fish right off the boat

🐟 If you're not a fisherman—or not a very successful fisherman—consider buying fish right off the boat. You can see the conditions in which the fish are kept and talk with the captain and crew about handling practices. Very often you can purchase live fish this way. Talk with others who have purchased fish right off the boat or ask bait shop owners for recommendations.

TIP 193: Proper handling of fish begins when they are caught

🐟 Freshly caught fish should be protected from sun or heat. Bleed dead fish immediately and remove internal organs. Keep fish iced, refrigerated, or frozen until you are ready to prepare and process. You can wash the fish in a vinegar and water solution to remove any slimy feel.

TIP 194: Consider lightly brining fish before canning

🐟 To produce a more desirable and firm canned fish, consider lightly brining the fish before packing into the canning jars. Mix 1 cup of salt per gallon (3.8L) of cold water and brine for 15 minutes.

TIP 195: *Leaving the bones in fish is okay*

🐟 Leaving the bones in most fish for canning is perfectly fine unless you're bothered about having to pick the occasional bone out of your mouth. Indeed, the fish bones should become soft over time and can be a good source of calcium. Likewise, leaving the skin on fish is fine too, although don't forget to remove the scales!

TIP 196: *You can pack fish in jars with the skin facing out or in*

🐟 Packing jars with the fish skin facing out is more attractive, but makes it more difficult to wash the jar for reuse. It's just as well to pack with the skin facing in for easier cleanup. Unlike the skin and bones, fish heads, fins, and tails are generally not the sort of thing that you want to can.

TIP 197: *If you decide to skin salmon, here's how to do it*

🐟 For some people, skinning salmon fillets is both a challenging and intimidating chore. However, it can be accomplished in a few easy steps. For skinning, the salmon should already be in fillet form with the head, tail, etc., already removed. Start with a long, well-sharpened knife. Lay the salmon fillet lengthwise, skin side down, on a flat, clean surface that is suitable for cutting with the tail end of the fillet on the right (unless you are left-handed, in which case reverse). If the fish is slippery, sprinkle it with a bit of salt so you can hold it more securely.

Slide your knife between the skin and the flesh at the tail end of the fish. Working slowly and carefully, continue sliding the knife between the skin and flesh, occasionally pulling up the flesh to check your cut and get a better grip on the fish. Continue until you reach the end.

TIP 198: *Be prepared for the fishy smell when processing*

During the course of the hours required for preparation and processing of fish your house is likely to be filled with the distinctive odors of, well, fish. It's not a smell everyone enjoys, so be prepared to open windows or light a candle. Dispose of leftover fish parts promptly and make sure the parts are wrapped securely. If you are disposing of fish parts using a kitchen sink disposal (don't place any bones in it!), run the disposal for an extra period of time and use plenty of water. Adding ½ cup (120ml) of lemon juice to the processing water might help to reduce some of the odor. Finally, don't forget about properly disposing of the fish scales. Although sometimes innocuous, the scales can punch above their weight when it comes to smell!

TIP 199: *Process fish outside on a camp stove*

You could also opt to do the actual processing outside on a camp stove. Small, single-burner camp stoves won't have enough oomph for the job, so you will need a powerful two-burner camp stove and use both burners at once. Make sure, of course, that you work on a very sturdy surface. It's best to choose a calm day since winds can extinguish burner flames. Have plenty of fuel to get you through the full processing time since any drop in pressure in the pressure canner will require that you begin your processing time all over again.

TIP 200: *Never use jars that are larger than a pint to can fish*

🐟 It is very important when canning fish to use jars that are one pint or smaller. Not following this practice is potentially dangerous because not enough heat builds up during the canning process to allow the destruction of *C. botulinum* spores, which can lead to botulism poisoning.

TIP 201: *Can oysters correctly*

🐟 Oysters can be successfully canned but the process for getting there is decidedly different than fish. Always use live oysters and keep them alive until it's time to can. To remove the meat of the oyster, wash the shells and spread them on a baking sheet. Heat them in a preheated oven at 400°F (204°C) for 5–7 minutes and immediately cool in ice water. Then you can drain, open the shell, and remove the oyster meat.

To prepare the oysters for canning, wash the oyster meat in water containing ½ cup of salt per gallon (3.8L) and drain. Fill hot ½-pint (240ml) or pint (480ml) jars with drained oysters and cover with fresh boiling water, leaving 1in (2.5cm) of headspace. You can add ½tsp salt to each pint, if you wish. Remove air bubbles and adjust headspace, if needed. Wipe rims of jars with a dampened, clean paper towel. Finger-tighten lids and process in a pressure canner according to manufacturer instructions.

TIP 202: Try canning clams

🐚 Canning clams is somewhat similar to canning oysters. Keep clams alive on ice until ready to can. Scrub the clam shells thoroughly and rinse, steam for 5 minutes and then open. Remove the clam meat while collecting and saving the clam juice. Wash the clam meat in water containing 1tsp salt per quart (1L). Rinse and cover clam meat with boiling water containing 2tbsp (30ml) of lemon juice or ½tsp (3ml) of citric acid per gallon (3.8L). Then, boil the clam meat for 2 minutes and drain.

If minced clams are your taste, grind clams with a meat grinder or food processor to get the right consistency. Fill hot jars loosely with pieces and add hot clam juice and boiling water, if needed, leaving 1in (2.5cm) of headspace. Remove air bubbles and adjust headspace if needed. Wipe rims of jars with a dampened, clean paper towel. Adjust lids and process in a pressure canner according to manufacturer instructions.

TIP 203: If you can clams, pay extra attention to cleaning

🐚 The simple fact is that clams are bottom dwellers that need sand and soil to grow. Cleaning them deserves special mention because even a bit of sand can make for an unpleasant grit in an otherwise tender clam dish. So take some extra time to wash the clams through running water and gently brush off the sand and mud until the water runs clear.

TIP 204: *Tuna can be canned cooked or raw*

⬤ Processing tuna can be a stinky business. Cooking tuna before canning removes some of the strong-flavored oils. Also consider only canning the more delicate, white flesh. There has been some suggestion, and practice perhaps, to use the dark flesh as pet food.

Keep tuna on ice until ready to can. Then, like other fish, remove viscera and wash the tuna well in cold water while making sure the blood drains from the stomach cavity. Place the tuna belly down on a rack or metal tray in the bottom of a large baking pan. Then, cut the tuna in half crosswise, if necessary. Precook the tuna by baking at 250°F (120°C) for $2^1/_2$–4 hours (depending on size) or at 350°F (175°C) for 1 hour. The fish may also be cooked in a steamer for 2–4 hours. If a thermometer is used, cook to a 165–175°F (75–80°C) internal temperature.

Refrigerate the cooked tuna overnight to firm the meat. Then, peel off the skin with a knife, removing blood vessels and any discolored flesh. Cut meat away from bones; cut out and discard all bones, fin bases, and dark flesh. Then quarter followed by cutting quarters crosswise into lengths suitable for $^1/_2$-pint (240ml) or pint (480ml) jars. Fill into hot jars, pressing down gently to make a solid pack. Tuna may be packed in water or oil, whichever is preferred, leaving 1in (2.5cm) headspace. Remove air bubbles and adjust headspace if needed. If desired, add $^1/_2$tsp of salt per $^1/_2$-pint or 1tsp of salt per pint. Carefully clean the jar rims with a clean, damp paper towel; wipe with a dry paper towel to remove any fish oil. Adjust lids and process in a pressure canner according to the manufacturer's instructions.

TIP 205: *Crab meat may not be your best canning option*

At the risk of discouraging the budding canner, you may want to consider freezing crab meat as a long-term preservation alternative instead of canning it. Canning at least some forms of crab meat can produce an acidic flavor in the meat.

TIP 206: *Know where your meat is from and how it has been handled*

If you raise your own food animals then you know each step along the way how the animal has been treated from raising to slaughtering and butchering. Not many people have that kind of information or control, so you must take precautions to know your butcher and ensure that all the safety regulations and inspections have been followed. *C. botulinum* is less common today but still possible and *Salmonella* is still quite common, particularly with poultry. Kitchen shortcuts or lapses in refrigeration and cleanliness could introduce bacteria that can cause nasty gastro-intestinal illness—or even death.

TIP 207: *Be particularly cautious—and especially informed—about canning wild game*

Deer, rabbit, and other game can be diseased or carry parasites. Your state fish and game department or county game warden can inform you about disease problems with game in your area, but you will still be dealing with meat that was raised in an uncontrolled environment. Bear can carry trichinosis. Rabbit can carry tularemia. Wear rubber gloves and thoroughly sanitize utensils and tools. Always cook wild game until it is well done.

TIP 208: Have a professional field-dress and butcher your large game

Butchering wild game is not for the uninitiated. How to skin, clean, cut, cool, and handle the meat are all major issues. If there is a wound area on the animal, there are additional sanitary and safety concerns in preparing the meat. An experienced professional knows the ropes as well as how to make cuts so that you don't end up wasting any more than necessary. It's a good idea to line this person up in advance so that your wild game is not spoiling while you are looking for someone to handle the dressing chore for you.

TIP 209: Don't be too anxious to get rid of all the fat

We have become conditioned to think that all fat is bad. Don't be too anxious about buying lean beef, though, or you may sacrifice quality. At least a little fat can add to the flavor and texture of the meat. Butchers talk about good, well-dispersed marbling as a sign of quality beef. Avoid meat that appears lard-like with a few islands of meat in between. If you're unsure of what good marbling looks like, ask your butcher for recommendations.

TIP 210: When selecting beef, color matters

When selecting your beef for preservation, look for those portions that are a rich red rather than purplish or pink. Beef that is grayish has been exposed to air or light, which indicates improper handling or curing.

TIP 211: If shopping for meat for preserving, consider specialty meats

⚫ Generally, commodity meats purchased from non-specialty outlets will be a lower quality of meat that may be less flavorful and more susceptible to becoming dry and tough when cooked. In choosing your meat for preserving consider specialty meats that are grass fed, grass finished, organic, or of the heritage variety. These will generally be more flavorful and will produce a better end product. Also consider premium USDA grades if purchasing meat in the U.S. along with whether the beef is dry-aged, both of which will also produce a better end product.

TIP 212: Avoid prepared meats

⚫ Prepared meats are typically of lower quality and have been dressed up with added flavorings, none of which may bode well for the quality meat product that you are trying to preserve.

TIP 213: Put fresh meats in your cart just before check-out

⚫ Plan meat purchases so that they are the last thing that you place in your cart. If you think there may be extended periods without refrigeration following purchase of the fresh meat, consider bringing a cooler and ice.

TIP 214: Don't forget the bones

⚫ Bones that would otherwise go to waste can be used to make meat stock that can be canned or frozen. To draw out more of the flavor, cut or crack bones to expose more of the marrow to the cooking liquid. Meat stock must still be processed in a pressure canner at the proper pressure and adjusting for altitude. Lest we forget about chicken or turkey bones—don't!

TIP 215: *Allow plenty of time for processing*

⚙ Recommended processing times for meat and fish are much longer than the few minutes of processing time recommended for most fruits and vegetables. Be prepared to process in a pressure canner for up to 3 hours or more, depending on the food and the jar size.

TIP 216: *Add extra water to the pressure canner*

⚙ The long processing and venting times required for meat and fish mean that more water from the canner is lost in the form of steam. Consult your owner's manual for recommended filling levels.

TIP 217: *Wash chicken thoroughly*

⚙ Recent news stories have advised against washing chicken prior to cooking because of the potential of splashing and spreading contamination. Well, that's for people who don't understand proper sanitation. Any kitchen interaction with poultry should begin with washing the poultry thoroughly. When working with a whole chicken, make sure you wash the cavity thoroughly as well. To paraphrase Sherlock Holmes, washing poultry thoroughly before use may be elementary; however, too many foodborne illnesses have resulted from not following this basic step.

TIP 218: *Ground or chopped meat, it's up to you*

🌀 Whether you're canning beef, lamb, pork, sausage, veal, venison, or yes, bear, it's up to you whether you want to can in either ground or chopped form. All of these types are suitable for both. If you are grinding the meat, it can be shaped as patties or balls or sausage links as applicable. If you are chopping the meat, strips, cubes, or chunks are fine for canning.

TIP 219: *It may help to know in advance the ratio of animal or fish weight to jar capacity*

🌀 When making your canning plans, it may help to know in advance how much animal or fish weight to allow for each jar that you're using. For example, for some forms of salmon, allow 2¼–3lb (1–1.35kg) of whole fish for each pint of canned fish. Knowing this in advance can help you plan better and avoid unnecessary expense, wastage, and most importantly surprises. If it sounds as though you have heard this kind of tip before, you did, in the fruit section. It's reemphasized here because no one wants to be surprised with a lot of leftover animal parts. With canning, like a lot of things in life, the fewer surprises of the bad sort, the better.

TIP 220: *Keep jar rings in place while packing jars with meat and fish*

🌀 Meat and fish have oils that can be difficult to clean off of jar rims once the jars are filled and before they are sealed. You can put the jar rings, without lids, in place while filling jars to protect the screw grooves. After filling, remove and wash the rings in hot, soapy water. Wipe jar rims with a vinegar-soaked paper towel to remove any lingering oils and residue. This will help ensure you get a tight seal.

SAUCES, CURDS, CONDIMENTS, AND CORDIALS

TIP 221: *Homemade tomato ketchups can be made without added sugars*

🔵 If you make your own ketchup at home, you can avoid the unwanted ingredients found in store-bought ketchup such as high fructose corn syrup. Tomatoes, onions, vinegar, and spices will make a wonderful ketchup all by themselves. It's up to you if you want to add salt and sugar. You can also customize and add to the complexity of the flavors in your homemade ketchup with ginger, garlic, coriander, fennel, allspice, cloves, dry mustard—almost any savory ingredient that strikes your fancy.

Allow plenty of time for ketchup making. Cooking time before bottling will take an hour or more so that the flavors can develop and the mixture reduce to a thick sauce. Plan to spend that time near the stove since tomatoes can scorch and burn as they begin to thicken.

TIP 222: *Mushroom ketchup is excellent with meats*

🔵 Although tomatoes get the majority of attention in the ketchup world, there are other types of vegetable, fruit, and meat ketchups, including cranberry ketchup, banana ketchup, and oyster ketchup. A savory ketchup that works wonders with all sorts of meats is the old-fashioned mushroom ketchup. If you're not sure you want to invest time in making mushroom ketchup without tasting it, search out specialty food stores and sample one or more commercial varieties. If you like what you taste, examine their ingredient lists and search out a recipe with similar ingredients.

TIP 223: *Grow horseradish and make your own sauce*

If you're a horseradish fan, you will love having the freshest available. It's easy to grow your own! Horseradish is made from the roots of the horseradish plant. It is a perennial plant, so it will return year after year. In fact, if you decide to grow horseradish, you should beware that many people consider it invasive. You won't have a little bit of horseradish. You'll have a lot!

Horseradish is harvested in the fall by digging up the roots of the plant. Don't worry, there will still be plenty to come back next year if you leave a bit. Wash and clean the horseradish root thoroughly. Slice and process the roots in a food processor with water, white vinegar, and salt. You'll want to wear protective gear, such as gloves and glasses. It's best to do this whole operation outside in the fresh air because the oils are potent and can burn your eyes and skin.

As with mustard, there is no need to process your homemade horseradish sauce. After bottling, keep it in the refrigerator and use within 6 months. But know that all horseradish begins to lose its characteristic kick over time.

TIP 224: *Experiment with different types of mustard powders, spices, and flavors to make your own mustard*

⬤ Homemade mustard is fast and easy to make. The basic ingredients are mustard powder, salt, water, and vinegar. A lot of mustard powder goes into making a jar of mustard, so plan to buy mustard in bulk. Know, too, that mustard powder brands vary significantly in heat and flavor. The Coleman's brand widely available in grocery stores is fairly hot, so if you prefer more mild mustards, be prepared to shop around for alternatives. When making your mustard, try adding a bit of wasabi powder (a little goes a long way!), horseradish, cayenne, turmeric, sun-dried tomatoes, beer, white wine, maple syrup, honey—the list goes on.

Since you won't be making several jars of mustard at a time, there is no need for processing your homemade mustard. Just store it in the refrigerator and plan to use it within about 6 months.

TIP 225: *Make a Southern favorite with end-of-season tomatoes*

⬤ If you have a home garden then you probably know the heartbreak of end-of-season tomatoes. These are the tomatoes that are everything a nice tomato should be—except ripe. They are green and are destined to stay that way because the tomato plant has given everything it has, fall is just around the corner, and the days are already getting shorter. In the South, those season-end green tomatoes get turned into a special delicacy: chow-chow. Chow-chow is made from diced green tomatoes mixed with peppers, salt, vinegar, and spices, such as mustard seed and celery seed. It is a mix between a vegetable and a condiment and is used to top everything from corn bread to pork chops to hot dogs.

TIP 226: Aim for smooth sauces

⚙ Any chef will tell you that strict attention to consistency and texture are critical to a quality sauce. Sauces that are meant to be smooth, such as barbecue or pizza sauces, should be absolutely smooth with no discernible bits of tomato, onion, or other vegetable that will affect the consistency of the sauce. Sauces that sometimes have bits of vegetable, such as marinara sauce, should have uniformly sized bits of vegetable and not have, for example, one outsized lump of tomato in an otherwise fairly smooth sauce. A stray chunk of habanero pepper in an otherwise smooth chili sauce doesn't just blemish the consistency, it's an unpleasant surprise when you're slurping up what you thought was nice and smooth.

Food processors, food mills, and those wonderful immersion blenders you can just plunge into the pot without having to dirty up a whole mixing bowl are absolutely essential to achieving the silky smooth effect you will want in sauces. Take extra time to blend and use a sieve to filter out stray bits that are too tedious to fish out of the sauce.

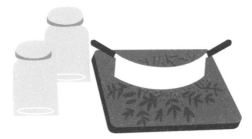

TIP 227: Take special care not to scorch sauces

Most sauces must be cooked and then reduced for maximum flavor. In the process, they become quite thick and can easily scorch the bottom of the pot, so regular monitoring and stirring is imperative to ensure you don't ruin a whole pot of sauce. If you do find that your sauce is sticking and fear it has scorched, immediately remove the pot from the heat and pour it into a heatproof bowl or other pot, but don't scrape the scorched bottom. Taste the sauce, taking care not to burn your tongue. If the sauce otherwise tastes good, then clean the pot of anything that has burned and return your sauce to the clean pot to finish cooking.

TIP 228: Give fruit curds a try

It's amazing the number of people who have never tried a lemon or lime curd. Fruit curds are wonderfully luscious custard-like concoctions of fruit, sugar, eggs, and butter. Curds are delicious on cookies, toast, biscuits, used in place of syrup on waffles and pancakes, or baked into pies and tarts. Frankly, they are lovely to eat at midnight while standing at the refrigerator with a spoon.

Because they contain eggs, curds should be immediately refrigerated or processed in a pressure canner. Experiment with making curds from citrus fruits, cranberries, raspberries, and mangoes.

TIP 229: *Use room-temperature eggs when making curds*

⬤ Eggs for curds that have been allowed to rise to room temperature will mix more easily and thoroughly with the sugar, butter, and other ingredients, producing a smoother curd. On the other hand, cold eggs separate more easily when they are cold. Since you will need more yolks than whole eggs in curd making, go ahead and separate the eggs you need for yolks and cover them with plastic wrap while all the eggs come to room temperature before using.

TIP 230: *Maximize the quality and flavors of your curds*

⬤ There are several small tricks that, added together, will help you achieve greater quality and flavor in your fruit curds. Be aware that the National Center for Home Food Preservation recommends the use of bottled rather than fresh juice because the acidity level is standardized. If you use fresh squeezed juice rather than bottled, don't let it sit around too long before you use it or it may become bitter. Squeeze juice just as you need it.

If your recipe calls for the zest of a lemon or lime, try to find fruits that have not been waxed to preserve them for display at the grocery store. If those are the only lemons you can find, give them a good scrub with fresh water and a vegetable brush. When zesting citrus, don't be so enthusiastic about the job that you get the bitter white pith.

By mixing the zest and sugar and allowing them to sit for a few minutes before adding them to your curds, your sugar will be infused with the lemon scent.

TIP 231: *Use a double boiler when making curds*

● Eggs are very delicate and should be treated that way. Using a double boiler rather than cooking the curds over direct heat will help ensure that they cook evenly and don't overcook or scorch. Don't overfill the bottom pot of the double boiler either. The water shouldn't touch the top part of the double boiler. A couple of inches will do the trick.

If you don't have a double boiler you can improvise one with a saucepan filled with a couple of inches of water and a stainless steel bowl or smaller saucepan that can be held above the larger one.

TIP 232: *Use a food thermometer to avoid overcooking your curds*

● Curds should be cooked, stirring constantly, to a temperature of 160–170°F (70–77°C). The only way to do this correctly is to use a thermometer, so make sure yours is handy. If you overcook the eggs, you'll have scrambled them and there is no way to salvage your curd-making project. You'll just have to start over.

TIP 233: *Make sure your curds are silky smooth*

🍯 Curds will be smoother if you use superfine rather than regular sugar. Superfine sugars are more readily incorporated into cooked foods so you will have less risk of a grainy curd. After your curds have reached the proper temperature, take the time to strain them through a sieve to remove any small bits of egg or citrus zest.

TIP 234: *Use several varieties of apples when making applesauce*

🍯 Apple varieties vary significantly in sugar content and tartness. Think about the apple flavors when selecting apples for your applesauce. Picking a few of this and a few of that type of apple may round out an otherwise one-dimensional applesauce. Naturally sweet apples include Red Delicious, Gala, Fuji, and Winesap. It is best to avoid tart apples, such as Granny Smith, if you want a naturally sweet applesauce without having to add a significant amount of sugar.

TIP 235: *Cook red apples with skins on to make pink applesauce*

🍯 That pink color of some applesauce comes from the red apple skins that are left on during cooking, infusing the sauce with a lovely rosy hue. Once the apples are cooked, the sauce can be strained through a sieve to remove any bits of apple peel.

TIP 236: *Add spices and flavors to liven up plain applesauce*

Kids might want their applesauce plain, but grownups will appreciate a more sophisticated flavor in this otherwise kid-friendly food. Cinnamon, ginger, nutmeg, cloves, mace, and even just a bit of honey will make the flavors more complex and interesting. For a truly grown-up applesauce, experiment with adding a dram of spiced rum or other adult beverage.

TIP 237: *Don't plan on canning your family's favorite spaghetti sauce without a pressure canner*

By themselves, tomatoes can be canned in a hot-water bath canner with the addition of a bit of acid, such as lemon juice. That's because although we usually think of tomatoes as acid vegetables, they actually fall in that middle range of the pH scale. It is the added acid in the mix that allows us to process the tomatoes with a hot-water bath canner. In contrast, spaghetti sauce has other ingredients that will affect the acidity, such as onions and bell peppers. These added ingredients are just enough to tip the scales toward a less acid concoction, meaning your sauce will not qualify for hot-water bath canning.

You have three options regarding spaghetti sauce. The first is to use a pressure canner for processing. You will need to consult recipes similar to your prized recipe to determine the proper processing time and pressure. The second option is to use one of the sauce premixes sold by canning supply companies that are formulated for use with a hot-water bath canner. It won't be your family's prized spaghetti sauce, but if you follow instructions, it will be safe. And finally, you have a non-canning alternative: Spaghetti sauces freeze quite well, which is perhaps the best option.

TIP 238: *Take special care when canning sauces with meats*

Sauces that contain meats must always be processed in a pressure canner. In addition, you should follow to the letter all the safety and sanitation practices for preserving meats, including using a proven and tested recipe, avoiding cross-contamination, keeping meats at below 40°F (4°C) until cooking, and cooking thoroughly.

TIP 239: *Watch for air bubbles that may hide in thick sauces*

It may not be as obvious that you need to check for air bubbles in sauces like you do with jam, but it is equally important. Air bubbles can hide in thick sauces, providing an environment where aerobic bacteria can grow. Ladling sauces carefully and close to the jar using a wide-mouth funnel will help to minimize air bubbles. As with jams, settle the contents and work a plastic knife or other tool into the jar and around the sides several times. You may need to adjust the amount of sauce in the jar to achieve the appropriate headspace.

TIP 240: *Make homemade fruit syrups*

🍓 Fruit syrups can be made in one of two ways. Fruits can be macerated—mixed with sugar and allowed to sit overnight to extract the juice. More often, though, fruit syrups are made with a process similar to making jelly, through cooking and straining to remove any fruit solids that could cloud the syrup.

Homemade fruit syrups contain a great deal of sugar to make them thick. If you try to reduce the sugar content by cooking to reduce and thicken the juice, you'll be concentrating the pectin. This may begin to set, leaving you with a runny and yet lumpy syrup.

TIP 241: *Don't can chocolate sauces, pestos, and other low-acid foods*

🍓 There are many recipes circulating for homemade chocolate sauce, pestos, cream soups, and butters. But the USDA's National Center for Home Food Preservation has declared that these low-acid foods are unsafe for home canning. Even using a pressure canner for long-term preserving is risky. You don't have to forego these tasty luxuries. Most can be refrigerated and used within a week or two. For longer-term preserving, freezing is a safer method.

TIP 242: *Make your own specialty adult beverages*

The beauty of homemade liqueurs, brandies, cordials, and sherries is that they are so easy to make. You don't even need to process them in a hot-water bath canner, since the alcohol does the work of preserving as long as the liquor you're using is at least 40 percent alcohol (80 proof). However, it does take time. After mixing alcohols, such as vodka, brandy, or rum, with flavorings, such as vanilla or coffee beans, almonds, or fruits, your homemade liqueur will need to be stored in a completely dark location for several weeks for the flavors to mature. It will be worth the wait.

Once the drink is sufficiently infused with the flavoring, you can strain it and store without the flavorings or you can just leave the flavorings in the bottle and pour.

TIP 243: *Stock your bar with homemade garnishes and bitters*

You know those lurid red overly-sweet maraschino cherries you can buy in little jars at the grocery store? You will swear off those forever after you have made your own maraschino cherries from fresh Bing cherries. You can also make your own cocktail onions by pickling wonderfully fresh pearl onions. Bar garnishes will never be the same once you make your own. You can even make your own aromatic bitters used in drinks such as Old Fashioneds and Manhattans, although it may require that you do some research to find specialized ingredients. The hunt is definitely worth it.

TIP 244: Make vanilla extract at home

If you are a baker, you know you can go through obscene amounts of costly vanilla extract in no time. You can make your own delicious extract at home using vanilla beans and vodka or bourbon. Slice three vanilla beans lengthwise and gently scrape the soft insides. Divide everything, including the seeds, into three clean bottles or jars. Heat 3 cups (700ml) of vodka in a saucepan for 5 minutes. Using a funnel, divide the vodka between the three bottles. Cover and store in a dark place. Each day for 2 weeks, give each bottle a small shake or swirl. After that, you can use the vanilla as is or strain into a new bottle for storage and use.

TIP 245: Experiment with herb vinegar combinations

Herb vinegars are made in much the same way as homemade vanilla extract, using red- or white-wine vinegar. Your own specialty vinegars can add depth and dimension to homemade salad dressings and other dishes. Experiment with different combinations of tarragon, chives, garlic, lemons, basil, thyme—you name it.

TIP 246: Alcohol is a useful preserving medium

Fruits canned in alcohol can make beautiful preserves. Some home preservers call them "gems in jars." The trick is to use spirits that are at least 40 percent alcohol (80 proof), the strength at which harmful bacteria and such can't survive. Gin, rum, vodka, brandy, and whisky all fit the bill. Preserving with wines, fortified wines, or cider is possible, but must be processed in a canner or have added sugar as a preservative. There is plenty of exotic fruit in alcohol recipes, but the simple ones—Boozy Berries, Drunken Peaches, Bourbon Cherries—are easy and fun. You can eat the fruit, pour the liquid over ice cream or cakes, or just sip it!

FREEZING

With little more than a refrigerator freezer compartment, the right food, and a container, you can get started preserving. It's no wonder that freezing is such a popular method of preserving food! Nevertheless, not everything can be frozen. And if a food isn't frozen properly, you might as well not have frozen it at all. Learn the techniques for preparing food properly and preserving quality and your freezer will be a treasure chest of good food.

FREEZING BASICS

TIP 247: *Frozen vegetables are still good for you, so freeze away*

🔵 While the literature is mixed, the first step of freezing vegetables—blanching them in hot water or steam to kill bacteria and arrest the action of food-degrading enzymes—does appear to cause some water-soluble nutrients like vitamin C and the B vitamins to break down or leach out. However, the subsequent freeze locks the vegetables in a relatively nutrient-rich state.

If you have access to fresh vegetables from the vine, you can minimize the loss of vitamins by waiting to pick them until they are fully ripe so they retain their full nutritive value. This will improve the nutritional comparison with their store-purchased counterparts, which may be picked prior to being truly ripe (although giving the appearance of being ripe) and that will be exposed to heat and light in transit which will further degrade their nutritional value.

TIP 248: *Freeze fruits and vegetables when they are in season*

🅢 As is the case with about everything else you do in the kitchen, always start with the best ingredients to get to the best product. The same is true with regard to freezing fruits and vegetables. Pick or purchase fruits and vegetables when they are in season and have their best nutritional value and then freeze them. After all, if you are going to go through the trouble of freezing your prized fruits and vegetables, surely you want a good end-product to eat. It does no good to freeze marginal fruits and vegetables in the hope that somehow freezing them will make them any better. It won't.

TIP 249: *Steam or microwave your defrosted vegetables rather than boil them*

🅢 It makes no sense after you have gone through the trouble of freezing your fresh, never-seen-better vegetables, to then boil the nutritional life out of them in a cauldron of steam and water. Instead, steam or microwave rather than boil your vegetables when subsequently cooking them to minimize the loss of water-soluble vitamins. After all, you do not want your hard-earned vitamins to go up in a cloud of steam!

FREEZER SELECTION AND CARE

TIP 250: *Choose the right freezer*

⚫ If your family has outgrown the small but convenient freezer in most home refrigerator freezers you have two basic expansion options: a chest freezer or an upright freezer. Chest freezers come in many sizes and open from the top. They are usually more energy-efficient than other freezer types, but reaching to the bottom of the interior compartment can be a challenge. Larger chest freezers also have a large footprint, but there are now smaller models with footprints as small as a refrigerator—or smaller.

Upright freezers offer easier accessibility and a smaller footprint than most chest freezers but sizes are more limited and they use more energy.

Either option you choose, pick a reasonable size for your family's needs since a half-empty freezer is less energy-efficient than a full one. An Energy Star-qualified freezer will use at least 15 percent less energy than other freezers.

TIP 251: *Locate your freezer in a convenient, cool location*

⚫ Two factors should be considered in locating your freezer. Convenience is key, since a freezer you have to reach by crossing a snowy yard is not apt to be a freezer you want to visit very often. Locate a freezer, if you can, in a place where you can easily reach it when it's time to cook. The other factor is temperature. Freezers located in garages that get hot in the summer or in warm utility rooms will be more expensive to keep cold. There may be no perfect location, so ultimately you'll need to weigh the merits and tradeoffs.

TIP 252: *Position lighting and a table or shelf near your chest freezer*

🌸 Not all chest freezers are equipped with interior lights and some may have fairly feeble lighting, so place a good light nearby so you can see deep into the bowels of the chest. From time to time, you may need to do some shuffling around to get to contents at the bottom or to reorganize. Position a table or shelf nearby so you don't have to plop food on the floor. If space is limited, you can keep a folding card table handy.

TIP 253: *Place your freezer a few inches away from the wall*

🌸 The back to your freezer should be a few inches away from the wall to permit adequate air circulation. This will also allow you to maneuver behind the freezer for regular cleaning and maintenance. Putting your freezer on appropriate rollers will also help when you need to move it around.

TIP 254: *Set your freezer temperature to zero*

🌸 Freezer temperature settings should be set to 0°F (−18°C) or lower. Not all freezer settings are accurate, though, so get a freezer thermometer, available at supermarkets and hardware stores, and regularly monitor the temperature and adjust the setting if needed.

TIP 255: *Use your kitchen freezer for short-term frozen storage*

🍓 Most of us open our kitchen freezer several times a day for ice cubes, an ice cream, or just to have a look around to figure out what to make for dinner. As a result, the temperature inside the kitchen freezer can fluctuate several degrees. When this happens day in and day out, the microscopic melting and refreezing encourages ice-crystal growth that can damage food and cause freezer burn. Because these conditions aren't ideal for long-term frozen storage, keep the refrigerator freezer for short-term storage of foods you'll eat up in days or weeks rather than months. That will also save your dedicated freezer for longer-term storage.

TIP 256: *Maintain your freezer*

🍓 Many—but not all—modern freezers are self-defrosting and require much less maintenance than models that have to be regularly emptied to remove accumulated ice and frost. Nevertheless, even modern freezers require some maintenance for optimal performance. If you keep a household maintenance calendar, add freezer care to it at the beginning of each season. Maintenance will include cleaning the motor housing, condenser coils, and grills to remove dust, dirt, and accumulated pet hair. Vacuum cleaners with brush and crevice attachments work well for this job. Check door gaskets and seals by inserting a piece of paper and closing the door. The paper should stay in place.

TIP 257: Defrost your freezer periodically

There is no glory in defrosting the freezer, but if you don't have an auto-defrost model, it must be done regularly or it will begin to resemble an ice tunnel and be less energy-efficient to boot. The frequency at which you need to defrost will depend on the conditions. Leaky seals should be replaced since they contribute to airflow that will cause ice buildup.

Locating the freezer in a warm space and excessive opening and closing of the freezer door will also make defrosting a more regular necessity. Try to time your defrost activity before a major shopping trip or freezing project. Defrosting takes several hours, so unload all the contents into coolers or into your refrigerator freezer so they don't melt or thaw. Unplug the freezer and prop open the door. If your freezer has a drain system, remove the drain cap and direct the water flow into a basin or pan. Place towels or rags around the refrigerator to prevent flooding the area and have a bucket nearby for squeezing and transporting dripping towels. Do not try to speed up the defrosting process by using an ice pick, which can damage the freezer interior, or a hair dryer, which can get you electrocuted. You can try instead placing a pot of very hot water inside and closing the door for a while to get the melting process started.

Once the interior ice is fully melted, wipe down the interior according to manufacturer instructions and dry thoroughly. Empty the drain pan under the freezer, if there is one, plug your freezer back in, and reload food from your coolers.

TIP 258: *Eliminate freezer odors*

🌀 Avoid freezer odors by ensuring that all frozen foods are well wrapped and sealed and that you use them by their expiration date so they do not spoil. If a power outage, leak, or other problem does manage to create a funky odor in your freezer, take steps to remove the smell. Remove and store freezer items in ice chests while you clean the interior of the freezer. Throw out any expired foods. Take out and wash any removable shelves, baskets, and bins as well as cleaning around door gaskets with a mild detergent. Wipe down freezer walls with a mixture of 2tbsp of baking soda and a quart (1L) of water and leave the freezer doors open and the shelves empty until the interior is completely dry. If you have a drip pan, check to make sure it is empty. This is also a good time to vacuum underneath and around coils where dust and pet hair can accumulate.

If odors continue to be a problem, there are commercial odor removers available at hardware stores. You can also try using baking soda or activated charcoal spread on trays in the empty freezer. Run the empty freezer on low with the trays in place for several days.

TIP 259: *Keep your freezer full—but not overfull*

🌀 Keeping your freezer full through regular restocking not only ensures you have a ready supply of foodstuffs handy, it also is more energy-efficient than a half-empty freezer. But don't pack in items too tightly because it can actually make it harder to cool since cold air needs to circulate evenly around objects being chilled. If your freezer is nearly empty or only half full, add containers filled with water to take up the space and increase efficiency.

TIP 260: Sign up to receive automated severe weather alerts

⬤ Advance notice of hurricanes, ice storms, and other weather-related events gives you to time to prepare for emergencies that can knock out freezer power for hours or days at a time. You can now sign up to receive free severe weather alerts that are delivered directly to your computer, telephone, or mobile device.

TIP 261: Prepare for power outages

⬤ If severe weather is headed your way, be proactive to ensure you don't lose a freezer full of food during an extended power loss. As soon as you know there is a possibility of a power outage, turn your freezer temperature control to the lowest setting. Fill bags with ice and tuck them into any empty spaces and corners of your freezer, including door shelves.

If the power does go out, keep the cold air in by keeping refrigerator or freezer doors closed. It's a good idea to tape signs to the doors to remind everyone to "Keep out!" You can take the extra measure of wrapping the freezer in blankets, taking care to avoid touching coils or other electrical parts. Foods will remain frozen for about two days, depending on the size and type of freezer as well as how full it is and the outside temperature.

Once the power is back on, take inventory of your freezer situation. Don't take chances. If power has been out for a while, use a food thermometer to spot check the internal temperatures of various foods in your freezer. All internal temperatures should be below 40°F (4°C).

TIP 262: *Use dry ice during extended power outages*

🌀 If power is out for more than a day and there is no end in sight, consider repacking your freezer with dry ice. Dry ice is the solid form of carbon dioxide and can be purchased at many grocery stores and some hardware stores. As a precaution, you may want to scout out a source in advance of needing it.

Purchase dry ice in small sizes since it is not safe for you to cut it up yourself. Place heavy cardboard on top of foods in the freezer and layer dry ice on top. Dry ice is extremely cold: −109°F (−80°C)! To prevent injury, always use gloves when handling and keep dry ice away from children. Once power is restored, simply leave dry ice in a safe place, away from children and pets, to evaporate. If you notice an odd smell in the freezer where you had stored dry ice, simply leave the door open for a few minutes and it will dissipate and disappear.

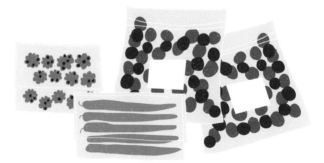

TIP 263: *Buy an easy-to-install freezer alarm*

A freezer door left ajar by a forgetful child who grabbed a berry pop can be left undiscovered for days. So can a broken circuit breaker or malfunctioning old freezer that has seen better days. For a few dollars and 5 minutes' installation time, a battery-operated freezer alarm is a good investment to make. The alarm is installed on the outside of the freezer with an internal probe that snakes inside between the seal. The alarm will go off whenever the internal temperature rises above a certain point. Some freezer alarms are adjustable, so you can set the temperature. Other models are even wireless—a handy feature if your freezer is kept in an outbuilding out of hearing distance.

TIP 264: *Refreeze foods—sometimes*

If a power outage has left your freezer foods partially thawed, it may be possible to safely refreeze the food, but many times it is not. As a general rule, foods can be refrozen if they still have ice crystals or are at a temperature of 40°F (4°C) or below. There are exceptions, though, and each item in your freezer should be evaluated separately for suitability to refreeze. Remember, if in doubt, there is no doubt. Throw it away. Always discard any freezer items that have come into contact with raw meat juices.

CONTAINERS AND PACKAGING

TIP 265: *Use heavy-duty aluminum foil and resealable plastic freezer bags*

🌀 It's important to keep air away from food while it's in the freezer. Air that comes into contact with frozen foods can compromise taste, change food texture, and diminish nutritional content. Always use products designed for freezer use. Aluminum foil comes in regular and heavy-duty weights. Use the heavy-duty version for freezing. It's thicker and less porous, making it less prone to ripping or snagging. Resealable plastic bags designed for freezing are thicker and usually have sturdier seals than regular food storage bags.

TIP 266: *Save time by packaging foods in boil-in bags*

🌀 Combine your freezer container and cooking container in one with boil-in or cook-in bags. They are great for freezing leftovers or anything else you'll want to cook quickly from the freezer. You can use them in boiling water or the microwave. Some people will boil several different packages of food in the same big pot of water to reduce cleanup time.

TIP 267: Remove as much air as possible from plastic bags and containers

⚫ Any air you leave in containers and plastic freezer bags can work to spoil food and cause freezer burn. Use the soft lids of plastic containers to burp out extra air by pressing down in the center before sealing. A clever way of getting air out of a plastic bag is to use a drinking straw. Insert the straw into the corner of the bag. Seal the bag as close to the straw as possible. Suck out the air and then quickly remove the straw and complete the seal.

TIP 268: Consider the benefits of an electric vacuum food sealer appliance

⚫ Vacuum food sealer appliances work by sucking air out of plastic bags and creating an airtight seal. They are a great way to quickly process large quantities of food. In addition, without all that extra air vacuum-packaged foods are often smaller than traditionally packaged foods, so you can fit more food into your freezer.

Whether you should invest in an electric vacuum food sealer appliance will depend on how much you want to pay and how much you anticipate using the product. Vacuum food sealers can cost as little as a few dollars to hundreds of dollars. There are handheld, countertop, and under-cabinet mounted varieties. Some are electric and others are battery-operated and even rechargeable. Most food sealers require special packaging materials, which add to the overall cost. You should also consider the fact that using a vacuum sealer doesn't eliminate the need for blanching and other safe food handling practices for freezing and thawing.

TIP 269: Allow ample headroom when using rigid freezer containers

⬤ Food expands when frozen, so if you fill a container up to the rim it is likely to overflow and push off the top as it freezes, making a mess. Depending on the size and shape of the container you will need to leave ½–1½in (1.25–4cm) of headroom.

TIP 270: Do not use unsuitable containers

⬤ Reusing household food containers such as milk cartons or cottage cheese or yogurt containers is a false economy. These containers are not moisture- and vapor-resistant enough to create the airtight seal needed for safe and quality freezing. Glass mayonnaise or pickle jars are not manufactured to withstand freezing temperatures and can easily shatter in the freezer or when handled. Always use plastic or glass containers labeled for freezer use.

TIP 271: Organize smaller packages into plastic bins or baskets

⊙ Avoid having to paw through dozens of bags of food packed into small packages to find what you want. Organize foods into small plastic bins or baskets. Hang laminated labels on hang tags so you know what's in each basket. One basket might contain stir fry ingredients or fruits. Another might contain soups or single-serving ice cream containers. Customize the basket arrangement for how your family cooks and eats.

TIP 272: Just say "no" to UFOs (unidentified frozen objects)

⊙ You may think you'll remember what's in that package you tuck into the freezer, but it's amazing how quickly you forget once it gets buried under the peas. Make a habit of labeling everything that goes into your freezer with a note of the contents and freeze date. The habit will be easier if you keep labeling supplies, such as a waterproof pen or marker, labels, and masking tape, in a drawer with freezer bags and other food storage supplies. Color-coding your food labels—green for veggies, red for meats, purple for fruits—can make it easier to spot what you want without keeping the door open any longer than necessary.

TIP 273: *Rotate food packages in your freezer*

🍓 Avoid expired and tired foods. When adding items to your freezer, take a moment to rotate older foods closer to the front so they can be quickly grabbed on your next visit.

TIP 274: *Take precautions to avoid freezer burn*

🍓 Freezer burn occurs when air slips around packaging and gets to the food in your freezer. Although it is not harmful to eat freezer-burned food, it results in a loss of nutrients, changes the texture, and gives food that disagreeable freezer taste. Avoid freezer burn by ensuring that foods are thoroughly wrapped and sealed closed. Expel as much air as possible from containers and bags before closing. Add an extra layer of plastic wrap over container foods before sealing the lids. Use freezer tape to secure wrapping so that it doesn't come loose over time.

TIP 275: *Don't commit your baking pans to long-term frozen storage*

🍓 To freeze foods such as casseroles and lasagnes, line the baking pan with heavy-duty aluminum foil before filling and baking, leaving 4–5in (10–15cm) of overhang on all sides. After the food has cooled, freeze it in the pan. Once frozen you can remove the cooked food and wrap for longer-term storage. When you are ready to heat and serve, just put it back into the original pan for heating.

HOW to FREEZE

TIP 276: *Blanch vegetables before freezing*

● Vegetables should be prepared for freezing by blanching to cleanse and sanitize food surfaces of microorganisms that can cause a loss of flavor, texture, and color. Blanching can be done either in a water bath or steamer. Some home preservers prefer steam blanching because it helps preserve vitamins and produces a better outcome.

Carefully wash, peel, and cut vegetables prior to blanching. Plunge 1lb (450g) of prepared vegetables into a gallon (3.8L) of boiling water. If steaming, place a thin layer of vegetables into a steamer basket and lower into the steamer with 1–2in (2.5–5cm) of boiling water. Cover the pot and process for the recommended blanching time. Water-bath blanching should be timed from when the water begins boiling again after the vegetables are added. Steamer times begin once the vegetables are in the pot and the lid is on. Always follow recommended blanching times. Underblanching can actually stimulate harmful enzyme activity in foods. Overblanching can compromise quality and nutritional content.

After blanching, quickly remove the food and plunge it into a large, ice-cold water bath to stop the cooking process. If the food is not completely submerged, place a plastic bag of ice cubes on top so everything cools quickly and evenly. Only keep vegetables in the cold water for the time it takes for them to cool or they will get waterlogged. Drain thoroughly before packing for freezing.

TIP 277: Undercook casseroles, pastas, and other prepared foods

Most prepared foods you remove from the freezer will go into the oven or otherwise be heated prior to serving. By slightly undercooking these foods you reduce the risk of overcooking them once they are heated.

TIP 278: Freeze food in small quantities

Take the time to divide food into small, single-serving quantities or in smaller sizes that can be combined for a family-sized meal. Smaller sizes freeze more rapidly and smaller ice crystals are formed, making the final product of higher quality. Small sizes also defrost more easily in the refrigerator when you're ready to use them.

TIP 279: Pre-freeze foods before packing and freezing

Soft foods can get mangled in the packaging and freezing process. Preserve the shape of items such as meatballs and pre-formed cookie dough balls by prefreezing before packing. Just spread the preformed foods in a single layer onto a cookie sheet and freeze. Once they are frozen, promptly package them for longer-term storage. This process also helps to keep foods such as green peas and beans from bunching into a solid block in the freezer bag, making them easier to remove a bit at a time to toss onto salads or in soups.

TIP 280: *Know how to layer individual portions*

● Separate individual portions of burgers, fillets, or other foods with wax paper before packaging and freezing. This keeps layers from sticking together and allows you to remove just the number of portions you need.

TIP 281: *Freeze foods as quickly as possible*

● Commercial freezing plants use liquid nitrogen to flash-freeze foods in seconds. This process helps to preserve food quality. The reason is that foods are made up of as much as 95 percent water, so ice crystals form when you freeze foods. If you freeze food too slowly these ice crystals can break through cell walls of foods and negatively impact the texture and quality.

You can't completely duplicate a commercial freezing operation at home, but you can take steps to make sure your foods freeze as quickly as possible. These include keeping your freezer well-stocked. Avoid adding too many foods at one time, which can bring down the freezer temperature. Freeze in smaller quantities that cool faster. Also, never add hot foods to your freezer that can raise the overall temperature of your freezer and foods.

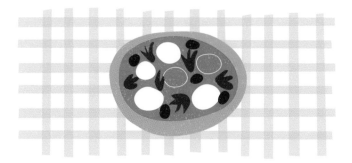

TIP 282: *Use dry ice to flash-freeze at home*

⚙ Commercial flash freezing helps preserve food quality by reducing the creation of large water crystals that can push through cell walls and impact texture and taste. You can come close to simulating commercial flash-freezing right at home with dry ice and a cooler. This is a great way to freeze blueberries, strawberries, and other delicate fruits that might otherwise get mushy in the freezer.

To freeze with dry ice, place dry ice in the bottom of a large ice chest and put on the lid for half an hour or more. Wash, dry, and spread fruit on a baking sheet that can fit into the cooler. Then put the baking sheet right on top of the dry ice in the cooler and put the top back on. Your fruit should be frozen within 30–45 minutes and can be repacked into bags or containers. Always follow safety precautions when using dry ice.

TIP 283: *Keep an inventory of frozen foods*

🞄 "Out of sight, out of mind" goes for frozen foods too, especially if you have a dedicated freezer and a significant quantity of frozen foods. Avoid having to throw away frozen meats past their prime or having to gorge on a season of peach pies in the month before peach season by keeping a running freezer inventory.

A handy way to make sure your inventory is always up-to-date is to keep the inventory on a magnetized clipboard on the freezer door along with a pen on a string. Jot down the food, quantity, and freeze date of everything that goes into the freezer and mark off everything as it goes out. Consult the inventory when planning the week's menus to ensure you're using your own quality foods.

TIP 284: *Keep an organized freezer*

🞄 Leaving the freezer door hanging open while you rummage around to find that last package of peas listed on your freezer inventory wastes energy and can bring down the internal temperature. To make sure you can make a speedy entrance and exit to get what you need, organize your freezer around food types. Group similar foods together, such as vegetables in one place, fruits in another, and casseroles in a stack. Consider adding labeled plastic storage baskets to hold smaller freezer bags and containers of single-serving items. Label food containers so they can be read easily without having to move or remove items.

FOODS FOR FREEZING

TIP 285: *Know what foods to freeze—and what foods not to freeze*

● Freezing is so fast and easy, it's tempting to double everything you cook to freeze for another day. The fact is, however, that some foods just don't freeze well, particularly some dairy products and high-moisture content vegetables. Foods such as avocados, cabbage, celery, cucumbers, lettuce, and parsley become waterlogged, limp, and discolored when frozen. Potatoes can become mealy and crumbly. Milk-based sauces, sour cream, and mayonnaise can separate and get watery. Meringue loses its delicate texture and becomes tough. Most fried foods will lose their appealing crispness and become soggy. These foods are best preserved in other ways or incorporated fresh into dishes before serving.

TIP 286: *Make extras when you cook*

● Freezing is the perfect preservation method for the time-stressed cook. Although canning and drying can take time, freezing a whole meal can be as easy as doubling tonight's casserole recipe and doubling a recipe doesn't take double the time! Marinaras, lasagnes, stews, and soups are all perfect for doubling—or tripling—when you cook so you can put extras in the freezer. When cooking foods such as pancakes or brown rice, make extras so you can package and freeze. Pancakes can be reheated in the microwave or toaster oven. Rice can be stirred frozen into soups or thawed and eaten, or used in other cooking.

TIP 287: *Freeze summer herbs*

🌀 One of the many wonderful things about growing herbs is that they grow nearly as fast as you cut them. You can easily store away a year's worth of herbs for cooking by regularly freezing anything you can't use right away.

It is best to cut herbs in the morning before the heat of the day causes the plant to move moisture back to the roots. Wash herbs by swishing them in cool water. You can blanch herbs before freezing, but it isn't necessary. Just wrap dried herbs in freezer paper or seal in a plastic bag. You can also chop herbs such as basil and oregano, mix with water, and freeze in ice cube trays. Once frozen the herb cubes can be popped out and sealed in a plastic bag until you're ready to drop them into soups or stews.

TIP 288: *Freeze your nuts*

🌀 Nuts contain oils that can quickly become rancid when stored at room temperature. Store shelled nuts in a tightly sealed bag in the freezer to extend their usability.

TIP 289: *Air-dry berries and other fruit before freezing*

🍓 Before packing and freezing strawberries, blueberries, or other fruit, allow the fruit to dry thoroughly. The water on wet or damp fruit will turn into ice crystals that will push through cell walls in the fruit, negatively affecting consistency. Air drying will also minimize their sticking together in the bag.

TIP 290: *You can freeze some dairy foods*

🍓 It can be quite handy to have a few sticks of butter or cream cheese tucked away in the freezer if you only use these foods once in a while. You can freeze many dairy foods, but you should expect some change in texture or quality and they're better used for cooking than for serving straight up.

High-quality salted butters made from pasteurized cream can be frozen. Unsalted butters tend to lose their flavor more quickly so the storage time is shorter. Herb butters and fruit butters freeze well. Hard and semi-hard cheese can be frozen. They will be more crumbly and dry than fresh, but are still good for use in casseroles and baked goods. Freeze cheese in small chunks. Cottage cheese and ricotta cheese can be frozen for a month. Cream cheese can be frozen but is best used for dips or as icing than for spreading.

Thaw dairy products in the refrigerator and use soon after thawing. Never refreeze. Margarine, whipped butter, milk, sour cream, yogurt, and buttermilk can be frozen, but the texture can become grainy or separate. These foods are best used fresh.

TIP 291: *You can also freeze eggs, if necessary*

🥚 Eggs keep very well in the refrigerator for a month. You can freeze them but the texture may be somewhat grainy, so you will want to consider how you'll use them.

To freeze, crack eggs into a container and thoroughly mix the yolks and whites, taking care not to mix in any air. Egg yolks and egg whites can also be frozen separately. Again, stir to mix without introducing air. You can reduce graininess if you don't mind adding sugar or salt. Stir in 1tbsp sugar or $\frac{1}{2}$tsp salt per cup of whole eggs or 2tbsp sugar or 1tsp salt per cup of egg yolks. Make sure to leave about $\frac{1}{2}$in (1.25cm) of headspace in the container to allow for expansion when freezing.

TIP 292: *Freeze baking and cooking leftover ingredients in micro-sized containers*

🥚 Some recipes call for small amounts of ingredients such as tomato paste, chicken stock, or pineapple juice. Unless you use these items all the time the rest of the ingredients can go to waste. Keep a supply of 2oz (60g) and 4oz (120g) containers on hand so next time you have leftover ingredients you can freeze them for use another time.

TIP 293: Homemade fruit pies freeze well

⚙ Whole fruit pies keep beautifully in the freezer for about 3 months. If you're freezing a whole pie, brush the whole bottom crust with egg white before filling to prevent sogginess. Do not cut air vents in the top crust. When it is time to bake, cut air vents, put the frozen pie into the oven, and bake at 425°F (220°C) for 15 minutes and then reduce the heat to 375°F (190°C) and continue baking until the center bubbles and the crust is brown. Custard pies, cream pies, and meringues do not freeze well.

TIP 294: Freeze pie dough or ready-made crusts

⚙ Have you read the ingredients list of refrigerated or frozen pie crusts in the grocery store? They contain ingredients such as hydrogenated lard, extra starches, butylated hydroxyanisole (BHA), butylated hydroxytoluene (BHT), and food dyes. In contrast, a homemade pie crust usually has about four ingredients—flour, butter or shortening, salt and/or sugar, and water—and only takes 5–10 minutes to make.

Pie dough can be frozen in a well-wrapped ball and thawed in the refrigerator for 24 hours before rolling out and using. Or go ahead and roll the dough out into a pie tin, place in a plastic bag, and freeze so it'll be ready to go when you are.

TIP 295: *Gain flexibility by freezing pie fillings separately*

One of the advantages of freezing pie fillings separately from the frozen crust is that you reduce the risk of creating a soggy crust. Another reason is that by freezing the filling separately you give yourself more flexibility to use the filling for another purpose, perhaps for a cobbler or to serve with ice cream or pancakes. Then the pie crust can be used for another purpose too, perhaps a coconut cream pie that you couldn't freeze.

TIP 296: *Don't forget to freeze summer treats*

Freezing isn't just for vegetables! Homemade fruit pops, fudgsicles, icies, ice cream sandwiches—all those summer treats we used to buy from the ice cream man—can be as close as your freezer when it's sweltering outside. Frozen confections can be as simple as filling an ice tray with fruit juice or puréed fruits. Or you can find frozen pop molds in an astonishing array of shapes. Try frozen fruit kebobs, chocolate-covered bananas on a stick, or frozen grapes.

Don't forget your dog. Frozen dog treats can be made from plain yogurt and bananas. Or try combinations with other fruits, meats, and beef or chicken stock. Grapes, raisins, fruit pits, seeds and some nuts are poisonous to dogs, so leave those out.

TIP 297: *Freeze individual serving sizes in muffin pans*

🍳 Mashed potatoes, macaroni and cheese, and other soft foods you want to freeze for individual serving sizes can be divided into muffin pans and frozen. Once they are frozen you can pop them out of the tins and into individual plastic bags to store in one larger plastic bag or a container. Soft silicone muffin molds make removing the food from the pan easier. Don't forget to label and date since it's easy to forget what you froze and when.

TIP 298: *Know how freezing affects herbs, spices, and other seasonings in foods*

🍳 The process of freezing can intensify some flavors, leave some less robust, and change some flavors altogether. If you plan on freezing casseroles, soups, or other foods that contain herbs, spices, and other seasonings, know what to expect and adjust your recipe accordingly.

Most cooks know that salt loses its flavor in freezing. Freezing can also increase the rancidity of foods that contain fat. Flavors that increase in intensity include pepper, garlic, celery seasonings, green peppers, cloves, and imitation vanilla. Onion and paprika change flavor, and curry can develop an off, musty odor.

TIP 299: Assemble your own ready-to-cook stir-fry or slow cooker freezer kit

🌀 A hearty stir-fry or slow-cooker stew is nutritious, fast, and easy to make. You can make the whole process even faster by putting together your own vegetable stir-fry or slow cooker kits in freezer bag serving sizes. Sugar snaps, green beans, carrots, red, green, and yellow peppers can be tossed together for a colorful vegetable combination. Freeze bite-sized pieces of chicken, beef, or pork in separate bags. You can even freeze rice, although brown and wild rice freeze better than white rice. Clip the separate freezer bags together or put them into a larger freezer bag so you can just grab and go.

TIP 300: Freeze sandwiches

🌀 Lunch sandwiches can be frozen for up to 2 weeks, allowing you to make a bunch of sandwiches you can grab on your way out the door in the morning. Don't make sandwiches with mayonnaise, lettuce, or other foods you shouldn't freeze. Peanut butter, meats, shredded cheese, and cooked vegetables work well. You can even cut the sandwiches into stars or other fun shapes for the kids. To keep your bread from becoming soggy, spread each side with a thin layer of butter.

TIP 301: *Make and freeze homemade pizza*

⬤ Making and freezing your own homemade pizza will save you money over store-bought or delivery and ensure you get exactly the type of toppings you want. You can use store-bought or homemade dough. To keep the dough from getting soggy, partially bake it before adding toppings. Wrap your topped pizza with plastic wrap and then with aluminum foil. Don't forget to label your pizza with a note of the ingredients and freeze date. Homemade pizza will keep in the freezer for about 3 months. To heat, just put your unwrapped frozen pizza on a pan in a 450°F (230°C) oven until it is golden and bubbly.

TIP 302: *You can freeze frosted and decorated cakes*

⬤ Wedding cakes, cupcakes, and other frosted and decorated cakes can be frozen using the open-freezing method. All that means is that you first freeze the cake without wrapping so that frosting won't stick to the packaging or get squished. Don't allow the cake to sit in the freezer for too long though or you'll end up with a freezer-burned cake. Wrap extremely well. Frosted cakes can be stored in the freezer for up to 3 months. Unfrosted cakes can last up to 6 months.

Avoid freezing cooked, boiled, or fruit frostings and fillings since they don't freeze well. Cakes freeze best if they are naturally dense and moist, such as carrot cake. Freezing will not improve a cake that is already dry.

TIP 303: *Give frozen ice cream an extra layer of protection*

Ice cream, whether it is homemade or store-bought, can get that funky freezer taste in as little as 2 weeks. Provide an extra layer of protection from the damaging air by layering plastic freezer wrap over the contents of the ice cream container before tightly sealing.

TIP 304: *Extend the life of flour and grains by freezing*

Storing flour and grains in the freezer can significantly extend the life of these foods and prevents any weevil larvae that might be in the grains from hatching and growing. Whole grain flours, in particular, benefit from refrigerator or freezer storage, because the germ portion of the grain can become rancid over time. The paper most flour comes in is too porous for freezer storage. Wrap flour well in plastic wrap and aluminum foil or repackage into an airtight, sealed container to keep it from absorbing moisture and odors from other foods in the freezer, which can affect taste.

TIP 305: *Defrost foods in the refrigerator in cold water*

⏺ The bacteria we inactivate by freezing can grow once you thaw your frozen food. Defrost foods safely by placing them overnight in the refrigerator, especially any foods that contain meat, fish, or eggs. Allow enough time for defrosting—at least a day for each 5lb (2.25kg) of weight for larger items, such as roasts or turkeys.

Foods can be thawed in cold—not hot—water if they are completely sealed in waterproof packaging. Monitor carefully and change the water every 30 minutes as the food thaws. Foods thawed by the cold water method must be cooked immediately.

TIP 306: *Take care when thawing in the microwave*

⏺ You can also defrost items in your microwave on the defrost setting, but the microwave defrosts foods very unevenly. It is possible for some parts of foods to be cooked and others still frozen. If you defrost foods in the microwave, plan to cook them immediately. Foods stored in plastic containers should not be microwaved unless they are specifically labeled for microwave use. Regular plastic containers may soften in the microwave and could leach chemicals into the food.

TIP 307: *Use caution when thawing foods at room temperature*

● Thawing meats, eggs, casseroles, or most other foods on the countertop or anywhere at room temperature is not considered safe. Although the center of foods may still be frozen, the outside of the foods could well reach above 40°F (4°C)—the danger zone at which bacteria can grow.

TIP 308: *Baked goods can be thawed at room temperature, but take steps to make sure they don't get soggy*

● Breads, rolls, cakes, and other baked goods can be safely thawed on the kitchen counter. The rapid change from freezing to room temperature, however, may cause condensation to build up inside the plastic wrapping, which can leave your baked goods a bit soggy. You can avoid this by unwrapping or at least opening the plastic packaging to allow the moisture to escape. Once the food is thawed, you can safely rewrap it without worry of excess moisture. Another alternative is to thaw baked goods more slowly by moving them to the refrigerator for a day and then moving them to the kitchen counter to come to room temperature.

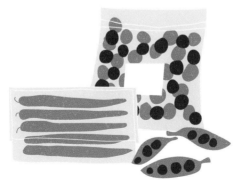

TIP 309: *Learn to make the perfect burger patty*

⚫ You can just squish out hamburger patties to put in the freezer, but there is a better way. The key is delicacy. Ground chuck makes a more flavorful and tender burger than lean ground beef.

To make the perfect patty, start by placing the beef in a bowl and then separating it with a fork. If you are adding ingredients to your meat mixture, do not overblend or it may overly compact the mixture and make the patties tough and dry.

Pick up a handful of the loosened burger and gently form the portion into a round ball, taking care that you don't pack it tightly. Then play a bit of catch by tossing the ball back and forth between your palms until the beef forms the perfect ball without cracks or crevices. Place the burger ball on wax paper and gently press it with the palm of your hand to form the patty, which should be at least ¾in (2cm) thick with rounded edges and with as few cracks and crevices as possible. This will allow the meat to be cooked evenly. Layer burger slices with wax paper to prevent them from sticking together as they freeze.

When you're ready to cook your patties, thaw them completely. Don't press them while cooking because you may press out the juices and end up with dry burgers.

TIP 310: *Liven up your hamburger patties*

🍔 Your frozen homemade hamburgers will taste like they came fresh from a gourmet restaurant if you treat them gently and liven up the taste with some seasonings. For a flavorful burger mix, combine 2tbsp each of salt, paprika, and garlic powder, 2tsp each of onion powder, black pepper and dry mustard. You can also add a bit of brown sugar, cayenne pepper, crushed red pepper, or Worcestershire sauce. Use 2tsp seasoning for each pound (450g) of ground chuck.

TIP 311: *Avoid vacuum-packed ground beef for hamburgers*

🍔 Vacuum-packed ground beef for hamburgers deserves special mention because vacuum packing the ground beef inordinately compresses the beef, which in turn produces a dense pastry-like hamburger. Pastries and hamburgers may have some things in common, but this should not be one of them. Another unattractive element of the vacuum packing of ground beef is that a manufacturer may use leftovers of several carcasses, which increases the risk of *E. coli* contamination.

DRYING

Humans have been preserving food by removing moisture since we lived in caves. It is a practical skill because the results are nutritious, long-lasting, and compact. Drying is also a useful skill because you can preserve large quantities efficiently, create healthy snacks for the family, and have a stockpile of food for everyday needs, camping trips, or emergencies.

DRYING BASICS

TIP 312: *Understand why to dry*

⬤ If you haven't previously considered drying foods as part of your home preserving repertoire, there are many reasons to consider it. First, drying foods is inexpensive and easy. You can use equipment you already have available at home (your oven!) and by investing a few minutes, be underway with your first drying project. If storage is an issue at your house, dried foods are an excellent way of putting food by since they won't be filling up your freezer and take up less storage space than jars used in canning. Drying foods also preserves more of the nutritional value than canning. And because dried foods are concentrated, the nutritional content is concentrated as well.

All of these reasons are great, but also consider some of the culinary reasons to add dried foods to your kitchen pantry. Kids love dried fruit leathers. Dried trail mixes are perfect to take along on outdoor camping, backpacking, and sports activities. Home cooks will appreciate having a ready supply of the summer harvest well into the winter months to add to soups, stews, and other dishes.

TIP 313: *Understand how drying works*

There are two requirements for successful drying: enough warmth or heat to draw moisture out of the food without cooking it, and enough circulating dry air to carry the moisture away. Removing the water in food deprives microorganisms, such as bacteria, yeast, and mold of the moisture they need to survive. The drying process also prevents enzymes from spoiling food during storage.

TIP 314: *Drying and dehydrating are basically the same thing*

You may notice that various cookbooks, websites, and experts refer to "drying" and "dehydrating." Sometimes these terms are even used interchangeably. Is there a difference? Scientifically, the difference comes down to a matter of percentages with dehydrated foods containing a lower percentage of water than dried foods. So officially, yes, there is a difference. But for the home preserver, not really.

TIP 315: *Dried foods offer good nutrition*

Dried foods look so different from their fresh counterparts you may wonder how the drying process affects the nutritional value. In the drying process, the calorie content of foods does not change although it is more concentrated since the overall mass is reduced once moisture is removed. The same is true of the vitamins. More vitamins are packed into a smaller package. There are some changes in the overall vitamin content, though. Vitamins A, thiamin, riboflavin, and niacin are fairly well preserved. Pretreating fruits with ascorbic acid or lemon juice boosts the vitamin C level, although some of that is lost during drying. Similarly, vitamin C is lost during the blanching and drying of vegetables. Nutrition is not the only reason to dry foods, though, so weigh the calories, nutrition, taste, and convenience and you probably end up with a pretty attractive package—of dried foods!

TIP 316: *Know the keys to successful drying*

Successful drying involves gentle heat of 130–155°F (55–68°C), continuous air circulation, and good ventilation. Using heat that is too high will cook rather than dry the food and could leave the outside of the food dry and the inside moist and vulnerable to spoiling. Without continuous air circulation and ventilation, moisture cannot dissipate and foods will not dry evenly. Successful drying involves creating the environment of heat, ventilation, and circulating air for a period of time—from several hours and even days.

TIP 317: *Know the advantages and disadvantages of open-air and sun drying*

● Open-air and sun drying are old-fashioned drying methods that are economical but not without some significant drawbacks. First among these is that successful drying requires warm, dry air. Open-air and sun drying isn't practical in cool weather or in areas with high humidity, such as the American South, or where rainstorms are apt to creep up and waterlog your drying efforts. Another consideration is that foods must be protected from birds, insects, and other hungry critters. Your drying project must be covered at night to protect the food from dew—and hungry nocturnal critters. Open-air and sun drying are not as sanitary as other drying methods, so that must also be considered when weighing the pros and cons of drying method options.

If you decide that open-air or sun drying is your best alternative, know that the results of drying by these methods are less predictable and that drying will take longer. Do some research to find plans for do-it-yourself drying trays, screens, and rack support systems. Whatever you construct, make sure you use food-grade materials for anything that will come into contact with food. Screens made from copper, aluminum, or hardware cloth can oxidize and leave a residue on foods that can affect taste and nutritional value. If you're particularly handy with tools, look into plans for making a natural-draft dryer, a kind of low-tech device that traps heat from the sun and also protects food from bugs and birds.

TIP 318: *Try drying in your oven or toaster oven*

You can use your full-size or toaster oven to dry fruits, although it is a little trickier than using dedicated drying equipment. Also, it can be costly to run a full-sized oven for several hours. Set the oven temperature to 130°F (56°C). If your oven controls don't go that low, set your oven on the lowest temperature and prop the door open. Spread foods on baking sheets and use an oven thermometer to monitor temperature. Don't use a propped-open oven for drying meats since the temperature needs to be carefully regulated for safety reasons.

TIP 319: *Pick a dry drying location*

Excess humidity can prolong the time it takes to dry your foods. When deciding where to set up your drying operation, think about the surrounding environment. The moist air of a basement or utility room will extend the time it takes to dry your food. Similarly, it will take longer for foods to dry on a hot, damp summer day in a house that does not have air conditioning.

TIP 320: *Invest in an electric food dehydrator*

An electric food dehydrator allows you to more carefully control temperature by providing some combination of heat and circulated air. There are dozens of models on the market ranging from very economical to extremely expensive. But you don't have to have a commercial-grade dehydrator to have a very good product.

Consider what types of foods you will be dehydrating and the type of heat and air you'll need to get the best results. Some dehydrators have temperature controls, but some do not. Dehydrators also come in circular and rectangle or square configurations. Circular trays give you less room to work with on the tray, particularly if there is a center post you have to work around.

Make sure that the stackable trays or removable shelves will accommodate the type of foods you're interested in drying. Some trays have holes to promote air circulation. Some trays are solid and have edges to hold liquids that can seep from foods during the drying process. Also, look into handy extras such as fruit leather sheets and jerky-making accessories. Finally, consider where you will place your food dehydrator for the sometimes lengthy drying process. Constantly running fans can be noisy and annoying.

TIP 321: *Closely monitor the last hours of drying*

As your foods near the end of the recommended drying time, be more vigilant at monitoring and checking for "doneness" so that you don't overdry the foods and potentially burn them or make them inedible. This habit is particularly important if you are using a dehydrator with a heat setting or your oven.

TIP 322: *Consider using a solar food dryer*

Solar food drying makes perfect sense in some climates. Solar food dryers can be purchased in kit form on the Internet. If you are a do-it-yourselfer, then there are also instructions for doing so also readily available on the Internet.

Whether you purchase a kit or you go it alone, consider these qualities in thinking about a solar food dryer:

1 it should dry food quickly;
2 it should have controls for venting and that allow for relatively easy adjustment of drying temperature and airflow;
3 it should be easy to load, unload, and clean;
4 it should be easy to set up and put away without a lot of fuss;
5 compactness and light weight should be among its features;
6 it should be weather-resistant and should keep the food dry in the rain;
7 it should be durable and be able to withstand variances in weather;
8 importantly, it should be pest-proof with all ventilation being screened;
9 the food trays should be made from nonstick materials that are also food safe.

If you are concerned about portability or are space-constrained, there are also forms of hanging dyers.

TIP 323: *Carefully choose the materials when making trays, screens, or racks*

⚙ Take care in selecting materials for making trays, screens, or racks that you are drying your food on to ensure they are safe for food use. Drying food on surfaces made of copper, for example, will destroy the vitamin C content in the food. Fiberglass surfaces may leave splinters in the food, while vinyl surfaces may melt in temperatures used for drying. Likewise, galvanized screen contains zinc and cadmium, which may cause an acid reaction that could form harmful compounds while darkening the food. Consult the many resources that are available through state and local agricultural extension offices as well as the Internet to ensure that your drying surface is a safe one.

TIP 324: *Let nature do the work by vine-drying beans*

⚙ Vine-drying beans couldn't be simpler. There is no special equipment or pretreatment required: Just leave beans on the vine to dry! Once bean pods are completely dry, sample a few of the beans by breaking them open and testing the inside bean for signs of moisture. If they are still moist, leave them to dry on the vine a bit longer or pick the beans, remove them from the pods, and finish drying them in a dehydrator or in the open air.

TIP 325: *Try drying sturdy vegetables on a string*

⚙ Bell pepper rings, mushrooms, and some beans can be dried on dental floss in the open air. Thread string through pepper rings or use a needle and thread to pierce vegetables and string them together. You can hang the string in a sheltered location or even indoors over a radiator or heating vent. Try making leather britches, a fun old-fashioned drying project. Leather britches are beans strung together decoratively for open-air drying.

TIP 326: *Pasteurize open-air or vine-dried foods*

Foods dried in the open air and beans dried on the vine should be pasteurized to kill any insects or eggs that made their way onto the food while it was in the great outdoors. There are two methods to pasteurize foods. One method is to place food in a plastic bag and freeze it at 0°F (−18°C) for 48 hours. You can also use the oven method. Layer food on a baking sheet and place in a preheated oven at 160°F (70°C) for 30 minutes.

TIP 327: *Think twice about drying meats and fish*

Meats and fish are moist and high in protein, a very hospitable environment for bacteria to grow. Nevertheless, people have successfully and safely dried jerky for many years and you will find many cookbooks and dehydrator accessories for drying these foods.

Extra care should be taken when drying any meat, starting with the source. In recent years, concerns about illnesses from *Salmonella* and *Escherichia coli* have led food safety authorities to question the safety of homemade jerky. You should recognize that there is a higher risk to safety with these types of foods. If wild game is used for drying, make sure that the contents of the gut did not come into contact with the meat. Fecal bacteria can contaminate meat.

If you are confident in the source and safety of your meat products, follow all possible safety procedures, including food handling, refrigerator marinating, pre-cooking, and storage. When processing, meats should be dried at a high, steady heat throughout the drying process—145°F (63°C) for 5–10 hours.

TIP 328: *Prepare meat for jerky making*

● Meat for jerky must be sliced very thin—no more than ¼in (65mm). To make slicing easier, partially freeze the meat to make it more firm. Trim away all fat, as it can become rancid. Slice the meat with the grain for a chewier jerky and across the grain for a more tender jerky. You can use meat tenderizers or marinades for a more flavorful jerky, but always marinate meat in the refrigerator rather than at room temperature.

You can also use special jerky-making attachments that come with some dehydrators for making jerky with ground meats. Jerky shooters are also available separately for use in making jerky in home ovens. Jerky should be dried at a temperature of 165°F (75°C) until a test piece cracks but does not break when bent—a process that can take up to 24 hours. Dried jerky can be stored at room temperature for up to 2 weeks in a sealed container. Increase shelf life and maintain flavor and quality by storing jerky in the refrigerator. You can also freeze jerky.

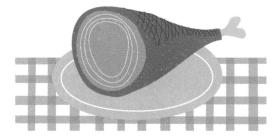

TIP 329: *Store dried foods in a cool, dry place*

🌢 Sunlight and heat are the enemies of dried foods. The higher the temperature, the shorter your dried foods can be successfully stored. Most dried foods can be stored for a year if kept at 60°F (15°C). Foods stored at 80°F (27°C) will last for only half that time. For best quality, use dried foods within 6 months to a year.

TIP 330: *Don't expect your dried foods to look like store-bought*

🌢 Homemade apple rings, banana chips, and other dried treats are perfectly delicious. But they don't really look exactly like the apple rings, banana chips, and other dried treats you can buy at the grocery store. Part of the reason is that it is impossible to duplicate industrial-size dehydrating operations on a small scale on your kitchen counter. But that's not the only reason. Commercial producers often add sulfur dioxide to preserve colors. Other chemicals as well as added sugars may be ingredients in store-bought dried foods. Beauty isn't everything, so appreciate your healthy, natural dried foods for what they are.

TIP 331: *Know how to identify problems with dried foods*

● Most problems with dried foods are easy to spot. If a dried food has even the smallest bit of mold, destroy the entire package. Dispose of any stored foods that show signs of moisture on the packaging or foods that have turned slimy or smell of something that they shouldn't. Obviously, do not eat any dried foods that have been infested with pantry pests. A simple rule to observe here is: when in doubt, there is no doubt. Toss it! There will always be a next time.

TIP 332: *Experiment and keep records*

● Drying methods, equipment, the water content in the food, and the surrounding environment where the drying takes place all vary significantly, so there are no hard-and-fast rules for optimal sizes to cut produce or for drying time. The best way to become skilled at drying—and to make your dried products tasty and attractive—is to experiment by trying different approaches and drying times.

Keep a record of the product, methods, and timing for each step in a kitchen notebook. For example, you may make note of the source of the produce, observations about quality and ripeness, cutting and preparation techniques, pretreatment methods, drying time, and environmental factors, such as air temperature and humidity. Over time you'll observe trends about what doesn't work very well, what works, and what works extremely well.

DRYING METHODS

TIP 333: *Carefully prepare and pretreat food for drying*

⚙ As with any preserving project, start off with the freshest and the highest-quality produce at the peak of ripeness. Take care to prepare foods properly for processing by discarding bruised or blemished fruits and vegetables that could promote spoilage. Scrupulously wash all produce to remove any lingering dirt, grit, or pests. Peel, pit, or otherwise prepare produce, cutting fruits and vegetables to a consistent size for even drying.

TIP 334: *For faster drying, slice foods thinner*

⚙ Smaller and thinner slices of food will dry more quickly than thick chunks or slices. It can make the difference between 2 hours and 2 days of drying time! You can get near paper-thin slices by using a food processor or a mandoline slicer. These are also excellent time-saving tools to use when making dried vegetable chips.

TIP 335: *Crack or "check" thick fruit skins before drying*

⚙ Some fruits have tough, wax-like skins that can make drying a difficult or lengthy process. To help things along for fruits such as grapes, plums, cherries, and some berries, crack the skins before drying. This is also called "checking" the fruit. To crack skins, drop the fruits into rapidly boiling water for a few seconds and then quickly plunge the fruits into ice-cold water. Drain well before any additional pretreating or drying.

TIP 336: *Pretreat fruits before drying to prevent discoloration*

⬤ Fruits that discolor when exposed to air, such as apples and bananas, should be treated with ascorbic acid or citric acid prior to drying. In most cases, treating other fruits is optional, but pretreating does offer some benefits. Pretreating can improve flavor and can decrease the drying time of fruits with thick skins, such as grapes and cherries. Pretreating also aids in killing any potentially harmful bacteria.

Ascorbic acid is powdered vitamin C. You can find ascorbic acid in some grocery stores or you can crush vitamin C tablets. Stir $2^{1}/_{2}$ tbsp ascorbic acid into 1 quart (1L) water until completely dissolved. Citric acid is also available at some grocery stores, but you can also use lemon juice or even pineapple juice. If using citric acid, stir 1tsp into 1 quart (1L) of water. For lemon or pineapple juice, mix equal parts juice and water. For either solution, soak the fruit in the solution for 10 minutes and drain thoroughly before drying. Do not rinse.

TIP 337: *Blanch vegetables before drying*

⬤ Vegetables should be blanched before drying to slow the enzyme activity that can compromise taste and texture, and also to destroy potentially harmful bacteria. Blanching vegetables also speeds the drying process, preserving the quality, color, and texture of the final product.

Vegetables can be treated by steam blanching or water blanching, but the USDA recommends water blanching because it heats vegetables more evenly. To blanch, plunge 1lb (450g) of prepared vegetables into $6^{1}/_{2}$ pints (3.75L) of boiling water. Cover the pot and process for the recommended blanching time, which differs based on the type of vegetable and how it is cut. After blanching, plunge the vegetables into a large, ice-cold water bath to stop the cooking process. Drain thoroughly before drying.

TIP 338: Don't mix different types of vegetables and fruits when drying

🌀 You may plan to mix several dried vegetables or fruits together after drying for mixes such as trail mix or for soup mixes. But don't dry fruits and vegetables of different types together on the same drying tray. Each vegetable and fruit has its own shape and moisture content that means it will dry at different rates. So, dry separately and then mix after drying.

TIP 339: Take the time to load your dehydrator carefully

🌀 Proper drying depends on good air circulation, so take the time to load your dehydrator the right way. Place food in a single layer, never overlapping edges as this will cause food to dry unevenly. Leave enough space between pieces for air to circulate.

TIP 340: Don't add to a dehydrator drying project in-process

🌀 Even if you have empty trays crying out to be filled, never add new batches of produce once you have started the drying process. Doing so will increase the humidity level of everything in the dehydrator and slow the drying rate for everything.

TIP 341: Use a vegetable spray—if you need it

🌀 Some foods will stick to the drying trays, making them difficult to remove and creating a mess to clean up. You may need to soak trays after use to get all the small bits of dried-on food left behind. If you find a particular food sticks to your dehydrator trays, use a light coating of vegetable spray. Don't use too much or you will end up with an oily mess.

TIP 342: *Condition foods after drying*

Some home preservers skip the conditioning step after drying. But it's an important one to ensure you have a quality product that will store well because it equalizes the moisture content of all the individual pieces and reduces the risk of mold growth. To condition dried foods, pack them loosely into glass or plastic jars and seal. Check and shake or stir the foods daily to resettle and redistribute any remaining moisture. If you see moisture on the jar or bag, put the food back into the food processor.

TIP 343: *Know how to test that food has finished drying*

Never package and store dried food without carefully testing that it is thoroughly dried. Different foods have different characteristics when thoroughly dried.

Dried fruits should be somewhat soft and pliable but shouldn't stick together. They should feel leathery and springy when folded. No moisture should seep out when the fruit is squeezed and your hand should still feel dry. Fruit leathers should be dry to the touch and yet still moist enough to bend without cracking.

Vegetables and herbs will be brittle. Meats should be carefully inspected to make sure they are dry throughout. Select several samples and cut through the thickest part to ensure there are no visible signs of moisture. If you notice moisture in a bag of dried food, it was not thoroughly dried and should be placed back in the dehydrator.

TIP 344: *Only use new food-grade plastic bags for storage*

Resist the urge to repurpose or reuse plastic grocery store bags. The U.S. Food & Drug Administration (FDA) requires that plastics used in food packaging be of greater purity than plastics used for non-food packaging. Food-grade plastics do not contain dyes or recycled plastic considered harmful to humans. Use only new food-grade plastic storage bags to prevent cross-contamination from previous contents.

TIP 345: *Label your dehydrator trays when drying herbs*

Once you walk away from the dehydrator you may forget that you put the parsley in the top tray, the marjoram on the second tray, and the oregano on the third tray. They'll all look pretty much alike once they're dried and you may mix them up. Either label the trays when layering in the herbs or keep a note of the order of the trays.

TIP 346: Dry herbs in lunch-sized paper bags

A fast and easy method of drying is to hang the herbs in lunch-sized paper bags to create a dark place and protect the leaves from dust and insects during the drying process.

Harvest small bunches of thyme, basil, chamomile, or other herbs, keeping the stems intact. Wash the herbs to remove any sand, dirt, or small insects. Shake or spin dry to remove excess moisture. Gather herbs into bunches and secure the stems with string or a rubber band. Place the herbs into small lunch-sized paper bags with leafy parts to the bottom of the bag. Gather the top of the bag around the stems and tie with string or secure with another rubber band. Hang the closed bags upside down in a cool, dark, and dry location. Basements and closets work well for herb drying in paper bags. You can hang several bags along a string or clothesline stretched between walls or shelves.

For best results, limit bunches to one herb-type per bag and keep bunches relatively small to allow for air circulation around the leaves. Herbs dry in a few days and should easily crumble into jars or bags for storage.

TIP 347: Try drying herbs in your microwave oven

Herbs have a low moisture content, which makes microwave drying in small batches possible. It is an excellent solution for people without dehydrators and who live in high-humidity environments that make air drying difficult. Microwaves vary significantly in settings and power, so drying herbs will initially be a process of trial and error.

To microwave–dry herbs, separate leaves from stems, rinse, and spin dry or pat with paper towels to remove excess moisture. Layer small batches of herbs between paper towels on a microwave-safe plate. Microwave according to manufacturer instructions or on high for 1 minute. Continue for 30-second periods until the herbs are dry. Do not overmicrowave nor leave the microwave unattended. Stop the process if you smell burning.

TIP 348: Get rid of herbs that have lost their fragrance

Herbs are supposed to be pleasingly aromatic. When you open a bottle or bag of herbs, smell them before using them in your recipe. If there is little or no fragrance to the rosemary or mint you have dried, it means they have lost their aromatic oils as well as their distinctive flavors. Toss them. They won't add anything useful to your cooking.

TIP 349: Only use food-grade desiccants—if you need them

If your food is dried thoroughly and stored in a dark, cool location, your dried foods should not require desiccants—small cylinders or pillows that absorb moisture from the air surrounding them. If you decide you want to use a desiccant, do not use silica gels or reuse desiccant packages that often come packaged with non-food products, such as electronics. Ask at your local pharmacy or search online for food-grade desiccants.

DRIED FOODS

TIP 350: *Consult rehydrating guidelines for your dried food*

🌀 If you decide to rehydrate dried foods, there are two variables to control: how much water is to be added per measurement of food, and the minimum time that the food should soak. For example, dried foods such as carrots and asparagus may require as much as 2¼ cups (500ml) of water per cup of dried food and will need to be soaked for a minimum of 1–1½ hours.

TIP 351: *Cook potatoes before drying*

🌀 There are better ways to store potatoes than by drying. They keep quite a while in a root cellar, for example. And even freezing mashed potatoes is better than drying.

If you really want to dry potatoes, they must be cooked before you dry them or they will turn black. Boil cleaned and peeled potatoes until they are *al dente*. Grate the boiled potatoes with a food processor or hand grater until they look somewhat like raw hash browns. Layer the potatoes on solid dryer trays for processing.

TIP 352: *Create a ristra to dry chilies*

● In the American Southwest chilies are often tied into bunches—known as "ristras"—to dry in the hot sun. Ristras make for useful kitchen décor that can use up the bounty of chilies that all seem to ripen at one time. To use, just pick the dried chilies directly from the ristra.

To make a ristra, select fully ripe, red chilies with stems intact. Green chilies are not ripe and will turn an unattractive ruddy color as they dry. Dry the chilies on newspaper or paper towels for 2–3 days to allow moisture around the stems to evaporate so they don't break when making the ristra.

Use a lightweight cotton string or twine. Select three chilies and wrap the string around the stems for three loops. Loop the string under and through two of the chilies, pulling it through the top. Make a half-hitch loop and tie it around the thrice-wrapped stems, pulling tightly. Continue this process using the same string, securing clusters of three chilies 2–3in (5–7.5cm) above the last set secured so you create a bunch as long as you can handle or as short as you have chilies to make. Hang a length of baling wire on a secure peg or doorknob, creating a loop at the bottom so that the chilies don't slip off. Braid two lengths of the chilies with the wire as you would a braid of hair, with the wire serving as one of the hair shanks.

Hang the completed ristra in full sun or in a location with excellent ventilation. Ristras must dry completely and without mold to be used as food, so air circulation is important.

Chili ristra

Twine

Chilies tied together in threes

Use red chilies for a more attractive ristra

TIP 353: *Make your own kale chips*

⬤ Have you seen the kale chips available at chic markets and served at upscale martini bars? You can make your own with a food dehydrator! Thoroughly slice and wash raw kale. Toss with a bit of olive oil, salt, lemon juice, and cumin. Layer raw kale into the dehydrator, avoiding overlapping ends of pieces. Dry at 115°F (46°C) for 7–8 hours or until crisp. Packed with vitamins and minerals, kale chips are significantly superior to the conventional potato chip in terms of nutritional value and can be a great snack that can impress friends and family alike.

TIP 354: *Use your oven to dry tomatoes*

⬤ Given the popularity of dried tomatoes, a means of drying them in an oven deserves special mention. Start by halving ripe Roma tomatoes lengthwise and scooping out the pulp and seeds that will slow drying time. Place the tomatoes cut side up on a cookie sheet and lightly salt them. Next, place the tomatoes in the oven; if you are using more than one cookie sheet, make sure that they are well separated. Prop open the oven door with something (a wooden spoon, wine cork, or some other device of your own creation might do). Using a temperature probe inserted through the crack in the door (a remote kind of probe of course will work best), adjust the temperature of the convection oven to 130–150°F (55–65°C). With that temperature, the drying time for the tomatoes will be 8–10 hours. The exact time will depend on the thickness of the tomatoes. The skins should look shriveled and puckered while the other side will appear dry.

TIP 355: *Pack sun-dried tomatoes in oil*

⬤ The wonderfully savory soft tomatoes you can buy that are packed in oil are called sun-dried tomatoes, but you don't need to dry them in the sun. You can use your oven or your dehydrator. After drying, loosely pack tomatoes in a sterilized jar. You can add sprigs of herbs, such as rosemary, thyme, basil, marjoram, or oregano. Pour extra-virgin olive oil to cover the tomatoes, making sure they are completely submerged. Push the tomatoes down and work to remove any air bubbles that may be hiding. Store in a cool, dark place. Wait for 2–4 weeks before eating the tomatoes. They will keep for about 6 months.

TIP 356: *Drying oranges and lemons*

⬤ Dried orange and lemon slices can make great garnishes or even holiday decorations. To begin with, evenly slice the orange or lemon into thin, even slices. If you are drying in an oven, preheat the oven to 200°F (93°C) and place the slices on a baking sheet that is lined with a non-stick baking mat or parchment paper. You may want to sprinkle the slices with confectioner's sugar to provide an added punch. Dry in the oven for around 2 hours. If you don't opt for the sugar on top you may want to flip them a couple of times. Alternatively, if you are using a food dehydrator, you will want to dry the slices for approximately 8–12 hours.

TIP 357: *Make cranberry raisins*

Dried cranberries, or cranberry raisins, are great as snacks, added to salads, or as part of a baking recipe. Because of their versatility, consider making dried cranberries a part of your drying effort. There are, of course, many recipes for doing so, but here is one to consider that starts with a 12oz (340g) bag of cranberries, 2qt (2L) of boiling water, and ¼ cup of sugar or corn syrup.

In a bowl, pour boiling water over the cranberries or submerge them in a pot of boiling water with the heat turned off. Let them sit in the water until the skin pops. Do not let the berries boil or the flesh will turn mushy. Drain. If desired, coat the berries with either a light corn syrup or granulated sugar. Transfer the berries to a cooking sheet and place them in a freezer for 2 hours. Freezing the berries helps in breaking down the cell structure, promoting faster drying. Put the berries on a mesh sheet in the dehydrator and dry for 10–16 hours, depending on the make of the dehydrator, until chewy and with no pockets of moisture.

An alternative method of drying is to turn on the oven for 10 minutes at 350°F (177°C). Then place the cranberries on a cookie sheet in the oven, turn off the oven, and let them sit overnight.

Finally, store the dried cranberries in the freezer.

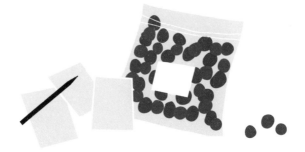

TIP 358: *Make dried plums*

Dried plums provide a lot of nutritional value. Two methods of drying plums include drying in a dehydrator, or, alternatively, drying the plums in the sun.

Whichever method you choose, first prepare the plums for drying by washing them in warm water, removing stems and leaves. If you are using a dehydrator, lay the plums on a dehydrator tray. Do not overlap or have the plums touching. Shrinkage will occur throughout the drying process. Plums will take approximately 24–36 hours to dry. To be considered dry, there will be no visible moisture and they will not be sticky.

Alternatively, plums may be dried in the sun after undergoing the preparation methods mentioned above. To do so, use two large screens of equal size, a piece of sheer fabric a little larger than the screens, and rocks or other heavy objects to secure the screens (the screens should be of a material that is safe for contact with food). Lay plums on the screen and cover with the sheer fabric and the second screen. Place rocks on the frame around the screen. Favorable weather conditions would be wind (at least a slight breeze), temperatures of 80–90°F (27–32°C), and lots of sunshine. These conditions would ensure the plums will be dry in 4–5 days. If the conditions are not ideal, the drying process can still be completed but may take longer. In the evening, put the plums in an airtight container and store in the refrigerator to prevent spoilage until the next drying day.

TIP 359: *Make sun-dried raisins*

⊙ Dried grapes—raisins—are perhaps the most popular dried food. They pack a powerful nutritional punch and can be eaten plain and in desserts, breads, and stews. If you grow or have access to good seedless grapes, you can squirrel away these little beauties to use for months.

You can dry grapes in the dehydrator, but why not try making yourself some sun-dried raisins?

Start with fresh green or purple seedless grapes that are as blemish-free as possible. Separate the larger stems and wash thoroughly, but do not remove the grapes entirely from the stems. Next, place the grapes on a tray that is wooden, wicker, bamboo, or plastic and that is slatted, so air can circulate around the grapes. The tray should be placed outside in a dry sunny place. This requires warm, dry weather. If your particular climate produces night fogs or dew, take the trays inside at night. Let them sit out in the sun for 2–3 days, or until dry. Rotate the fruit and/or trays to ensure even exposure to the sun. Remove dried grapes gently from the remaining stems and store in a dry airtight container in a cool place.

TIP 360: *Drying apricots*

⬤ Apricots may be one of the best fruits for drying. Apricots are an excellent source of vitamin A, vitamin C, iron, potassium, and fiber. Select firm, ripe apricots with deep yellow-to-orange color. To prepare, wash the apricots, cut them in half, and remove the pits. There are various methods for pretreating the apricots, such as blanching in syrup, that you may want to consider (and are available on the Internet) and that may produce a better product.

Apricots may be dried using a dehydrator, in the sun, or in the oven. If using a dehydrator, the average drying time for apricot halves is 18–24 hours. Sun-drying apricots requires low humidity, sunshine, and temperatures above 98°F (32°C). Place trays in an area that receives direct sun for as many hours as possible. Arrange the trays so air can circulate above and below the fruit. Cover trays with cheesecloth or a screen suspended above to protect the fruit. The average drying time for apricot halves in the sun is 2–4 days.

When drying apricots using the oven method, set the temperature at the lowest setting, preferably 150°F (65°C) or less. Leave the oven door open 2–3in (5–7.5cm) (block open if necessary). Place a small fan to the side of the oven door blowing inward to help remove the moist air. The average drying time for apricots in the oven is 24–36 hours. To determine when apricots are dry, remove a piece and allow it to cool. The apricots should be pliable and no moisture should be visible when a cut edge is pressed. Dried apricots can be frozen or vacuum-packed.

TIP 361: *Making banana chips*

Using a dehydrator or the oven are two means of drying banana chips. Start with ripe bananas (or at least nearly so) and slice the bananas into thin chips, approximately ⅕in (5mm) thick. You can treat them with lemon juice or some other acid if you are concerned about keeping the chips from overly browning. Using the dehydrator, dry the chips at 130°F (55°C) until they are slightly pliable or perhaps crispy, if that is how you like them. Store in an airtight container after cooling.

If you oven dry, place the sliced chips on a cookie sheet lined with parchment paper. You may also want to brush with lemon juice as noted above. Bake at 200°F (93°C), or lower if possible, for approximately 1½ hours. After cooling, store in an airtight container.

TIP 362: *Avoid all the additives by drying your own popping corn*

Some nutritionists have called popcorn the perfect snack food because it is a whole grain, a good source of fiber, and low in fat—that is, if you can refrain from adding lots of butter. By one estimate, Americans consume as much as 16 billion quarts (15.1 billion liters) of popcorn each year, which equates to approximately 51qt (48L) per woman, man, and child. If you want to keep pace, whether you live in the U.S. or not, then you may want to consider adding popping corn to your dried foods supply. You can store lots of the kernels in a confined space and have a tasty snack that everyone will love.

Unfortunately, store-bought popcorn has lots of additives, such as diacetyl, artificial colorings, and flavorings. Microwaveable popcorns have an even longer list of mystery ingredients and even trans fats. But you can dry your own corn for popping at home. Whether you are growing or buying popping corn kernels, make sure that it is popping corn and not one of the other types of corn kernel that are not suited for popping.

TIP 363: *Make sure you choose popping corn kernels and find the best types of popping corn that suit your tastes*

Believe it or not, you have lots of options when choosing popping corn—taste, texture, size, and even the color of the popped corn. Many popping corns have wonderfully exotic names. If you are growing the popping corn kernels from seed, investigate the huge variety of these seeds available from specialty seed suppliers on the Internet.

For home drying, Japanese Hull-less, Hybrid South American Mushroom, Creme Puff Hybird, White Cloud, and Dynamite are considered some of the best varieties. Also, for example, there are the Ruby Red and Strawberry varieties, which after they are popped have a white color with red speckles. There is another variety, Mini-Blue, which has dark blue speckles. If you are into multicolored popcorn, there is even a variety referred to as Cutie Pops.

If the shape of the popped corn is your priority, then there is, for example, the Mushroom variety, which is more rounded in shape and thus easier to add coatings to, while the Butterfly variety of kernel produces a more fluffy appearance. Related to this are some kernels such as the Pearl White variety, which have a relatively high expansion rate that produces a fluffy appearance with a milder corn flavor.

On the other hand, if you are looking for a more pronounced corn taste, plain yellow kernels may be your thing. So, shop around in deciding on the popping kernel that best suits you while considering those varieties that may be best for home drying. While perhaps not on a level with wine, at least not yet, popping corn has its own culture of taste.

TIP 364: *Choose the method of drying and storing the popping corn kernels that best suits your circumstance*

There are generally two ways to dry popcorn. You can shell it for drying or leave it on the ear for storing. The most important consideration in selecting the method may come down to how much space you have for storage. Either way, the prime consideration is to ensure that it is properly dried. Popcorn must be very dry—with moisture content no more than 13–14 percent—or the added moisture will negatively affect the ability to POP!

To dry popcorn on the cob, place the ears of corn in mesh bags and hang in a warm, dry, ventilated location. You can also place the ears of corn in a single layer in a dry, airy room for several weeks out of direct sunlight. Once or twice a week, shell a few kernels and try popping them. When the test kernels are popping well and tasting good, shell and store the rest of the kernels. If the popcorn is chewy, or the popped kernels are jagged, the kernels are still too wet and need to continue drying. The kernels should be stored in airtight containers in a cool, dark place. Glass jars with tightly fitting lids or the zip variety of plastic storage bags are suited for this purpose.

An alternative method is to store the unshelled corn on the ears in an airtight container.

TIP 365: *If you are harvesting popping corn, allow the kernels to dry in the field or garden as long as possible*

⬤ Popping corn can be grown in a field or garden environment. The important consideration is that, when harvested, the kernels should be hard and the husks completely dry.

TIP 366: *Don't forget about dried apple fruit chips*

⬤ Dried apples make delicious fruit chips. They are a relatively easy-to-make flavorful snack that can be easily overlooked in your menu or party planning. The good news is that there are a number of ways to dry apples, whether you use a food dehydrator, an oven, a wood stove, or the plain old sun. To make your dried apples extra special, sprinkle them with a bit of cinnamon before drying.

TIP 367: *Make your own garlic and onion powders*

Although most cooks prefer fresh garlic and onions, sometimes you just run out. And some recipes call for garlic or onion powders because they can infuse the flavor throughout foods that are meant to be creamy or smooth. Rather than buying store-bought, use a spice mill or mortar and pestle to crush your own fresh garlic and onion powder as you need it.

TIP 368: *Make fruit powders to use as flavorings*

Any dehydrated fruit can be ground into a powder that can be used as a food flavoring. Fruit powders can be sprinkled on morning cereal, added to icings and frostings, used in meat rubs, or included in candy confections. It's amazing how many uses you can find for flavorful fruit powders if you have them to hand.

To make fruit powder, freeze the dried fruit and then process in a food processor, spice mill, or blender. This is a very good use for fruit you accidentally overdried. Store in an airtight jar in your refrigerator.

TIP 369: *Make fruit leathers for the kids*

Rolled fruit treats you can buy in cartoon-printed boxes at the grocery store hardly resemble the original fruits. They are highly processed and contain corn syrup, food dyes, and hydrogenated oils—not things most parents want to feed their kids. Homemade fruit leathers are the tastier, naturally colorful, more nutritious food. Happily, they are quite easy to make. Fruit leathers are made with raw or cooked, puréed fruit that is dried in sheets on trays and then rolled for packing and storing. You can add honey, cinnamon, nutmeg, or other flavors. You can mix and match fruits too.

Try making a berry bomb roll-up by combining raspberries, strawberries, and blueberries. Cook 2 cups of raspberries in a saucepan until they break down and then run them through a food mill to remove seeds. Add 3 cups of strawberries and a cup of blueberries and continue cooking for 5–10 minutes. Add the juice of one lemon and ½ cup of honey. Follow the instructions for drying that come with your food dehydrator. If you're drying the fruit leather in an oven, heat the oven to 160°F (70°C). Line a baking tray with parchment paper, foil, or plastic wrap and pour on the fruit mixture, until it runs to the sides but doesn't reach them. You may need to use more than one tray, depending on the size. Heat in the oven for about 6 hours.

Your berry bomb roll-up is finished when you can touch the leather without leaving an indentation. Peel the leathers while still warm, cut, and transfer to sheets of plastic wrap 2in (5cm) longer on each side than the leather. After they are completely cooled, roll up the leathers with the plastic wrap. Store in an airtight container in a cool place. They can be stored at room temperature for 4–6 weeks, and will keep for several months in the refrigerator and up to a year in the freezer.

TIP 370: Try different chilies for different levels of heat

Not all chilies have the same level of heat. You can mix hot and less hot chilies to get your own special blend. Consult the Scoville Scale to see the wondrous selection of chilies to choose from. The Scoville Scale, named after its inventor, American pharmacist Wilbur Scoville, measures the capsaicin per unit of dry mass. Capsaicin is the naturally occurring chemical irritant that gives peppers their heat. The higher the unit number, the hotter the pepper. For many years the chili with the highest rating was the Ghost Pepper (Bhut Jolokia), said to be 400 times hotter than Tabasco® sauce. In 2012, the Trinidad Moruga Scorpion was declared the hottest pepper, measuring between $1\frac{1}{2}$ and 2 million Scoville units!

TIP 371: Homemade chili powders let you determine the heat

The chili powders you can buy at the grocery store are actually a combination of different types of chilies and spices, not just one chili pepper type. That's why different chili powder brands can taste like completely different products—because they are! Why not make your own chili powder to fit your special tastes? Try any dried combination of dried peppers and add ingredients such as cumin seeds, garlic powder, oregano, and chipotle peppers. After the ingredients are dried, just mix and pulverize to a powder in a food processor, spice mill, or with a mortar and pestle. Store in a dark place in an airtight jar.

TIP 372: *Recrisp crackers, chips, and cookies in the food dehydrator*

🌸 Placing foods in the dehydrator for about an hour will restore the snap to crackers, chips, and other foods that have absorbed moisture and would otherwise be thrown away.

TIP 373: *Dry and roast sunflower seeds*

🌸 Sunflower seeds can be difficult to remove from the seed head until they are dry, so let sunflower seeds dry right on the seed head. Of course, you'll have to cover the seed heads with cheesecloth or plastic mesh to keep the birds from helping themselves or cut it off and move it to a bird-free location. Once the seed head is completely dry you can rub the seeds right off. You'll need to meticulously pick out the seeds from any chaff that comes off with the seeds.

If you like the salted and roasted flavor of sunflower seeds, soak seeds in a brine of water and salt overnight. The amount of salt will depend on your taste. Drain the seeds and dry in thin layers on baking sheets in the oven at 200°F (95°C) until they are completely dry. Never eat seeds from flowers that have been sprayed with pesticides or other chemicals.

TIP 374: Roast your own pumpkin seeds

Roasted pumpkin seeds for snacking will involve two separate processes: drying and then roasting. Start with perfectly clean pumpkin seeds. Dry the seeds in the sun or in a dehydrator at 120°F (50°C) for 3–4 hours. You can also dry seeds in an oven set at 175°F (80°C). Stir seeds frequently to keep them from scorching. After the seeds are dried, toss them with a small amount of oil, salt, and other flavors and spread them in a thin layer on a baking sheet. Roast at 250°F (120°C) for 10–15 minutes.

Try different flavors on your pumpkin seeds such as Worcestershire sauce, lemon pepper, or a spicy combination of cayenne pepper, thyme, salt, and pepper.

TIP 375: Allow time to reconstitute fruits

Dried fruits you plan to eat as is should be reconstituted several hours before you plan to eat them. Reconstitute fruits by pouring boiling water over the fruit in a heatproof bowl. Add only enough water to cover the fruit. You can add more, if needed, as the fruit soaks up the water. Adding too much water will only waterlog your dried fruit and dilute the natural juices. If you plan to use the reconstituted fruit in a cooked dish, wait until the fruit is tender before using, which could take several hours.

TIP 376: Savor the beauty of summer all year long with edible dried flowers

Many flowers are edible and can provide a surprise bit of color in a salad or on desserts. Try flowers such as lavender, hibiscus, violets, roses, pansies, nasturtiums, marigolds, borage, and chamomile. Don't forget that some flowers, such as foxgloves, are poisonous. Select organically-grown blooming flowers without spots or blemishes. Avoid store-bought flowers that may be treated with pesticides or other chemicals.

To dry, remove stems and spread the flowers on paper towels in a breeze-free location. The flowers should not touch so air can circulate around the delicate petals. Alternatively, dry flowers on a low setting in the dehydrator, checking regularly as drying times will vary depending on flower type and quantity.

TIP 377: Try crystallizing flowers for decorative uses

Another way to preserve flowers is by crystallizing them—a perfect decoration for use on cakes and other desserts. Crystallize fresh flowers by painting them with 1 tbsp of gum arabic mixed with 2 tbsp (30ml) of rose water or orange flower water, both of which are available from some specialty supply stores. You can also use egg white, although you cannot store the flowers made this way as long as those made with gum arabic.

Be absolutely meticulous about painting the flowers inside and out. While still wet, sprinkle flowers with a generous supply of superfine sugar. Shake off excess sugar and dry on a wire rack. Store flowers very loosely packed in an airtight container in a dark, cool place.

TIP 378: *Make your own gourmet bouquet garni*

🌿 *Bouquet garni* is French for "garnished bouquet." Made fresh, these flavorful herbs are bundled and added to meats, vegetables, and soups, and removed after cooking. You can make *bouquet garni* from dried herbs by using small muslin bags purchased through culinary supply stores or just by bundling small amounts in cheesecloth secured with baking string.

There is no set recipe, but traditional mixes include parsley, thyme, bay leaf, and rosemary. Experiment with quantities and proportions to make the mixture your own special recipe. You can store the *bouquet garni* mix in bulk in a decorative crock or jar or in pre-filled bags or cheesecloth. They make a wonderful gift.

TIP 379: *Create your own herb meat rubs*

🌿 With herbs rolling in from the garden by the basket full, don't forget you can mix and match them to make unique and delicious rubs for meats and poultry. For poultry, try combining dried lemon thyme, sage, rosemary, salt, and pepper. For beef, try a combination of dried thyme, sage, marjoram, garlic and onion powders, pepper, and salt.

TIP 380: *Add custom flavors to your jerky*

● You can make plain jerky or you can make a wide range of flavored jerky by using marinades. Experiment with soy sauce, Worcestershire sauce, honey, corn syrup, beer, teriyaki sauce, Tabasco sauce, sesame oil, and even brewed coffee as liquids in marinades. Spices can include onion and garlic powders, red pepper flakes, cayenne pepper—even cinnamon and sugar.

TIP 381: *Make your own granola using your dried fruits*

● Homemade granola is a luxury that's easy to make. Mix together ½lb (225g) of chopped dried fruit mix, ½lb chopped nuts, and a pound (450g) of rolled oats with ⅔ cup canola oil, ½ cup water, and a cup of honey. Spread the mixture on baking sheets and bake at 325°F (165°C) for 10 minutes or until toasted. Store in an airtight container for up to 2 months or freeze for up to 6 months. Your homemade granola will be a world-class, terrific treat that will surpass anything you can buy in a store.

TIP 382: *Dry garlic and onions separately*

● The strong flavors of garlic and onions can be absorbed by other foods in the drying process. Always dry these foods separately to avoid giving other foods a garlic or onion smell and taste. After all, no one wants to, for example, bite into the homemade granola that you have proudly served up only to have it taste like a clove of garlic.

TIP 383: *Make chocolate-dipped dried fruit treats*

Everything is better with chocolate! If you are having a difficult time getting the kids to give dried fruit a try as a healthy alternative to processed foods, give them a little dried fruit dipped in chocolate. Dried banana chips become gourmet treats when coated with chocolate. The same goes for blueberries, cherries, figs—you name it. They also make the kind of gift that people will remember and ask for again and again.

After fruits are thoroughly dried and cooled, dip them in dipping chocolate you can buy in the produce or bakery section of your grocery store. Or make your own dipping chocolate by melting $1\frac{1}{2}$ cups of semi-sweet chocolate chips with 2tbsp of vegetable shortening. Stir thoroughly before dipping the fruit. Berries or other small fruits can be stirred with the chocolate and poured onto wax paper. The chocolate coating will dry more quickly if you chill the fruit before dipping. Let the fruit dry on waxed paper.

TIP 384: *Create dinner-in-a-jar meals to save time*

Combining or layering different dried foods together in large canning jars will look pretty impressive on your pantry shelf. But what's more impressive is how easy and convenient these dinner-in-a-jar meals can be on nights when you can't muster up the energy for the washing, peeling, and chopping to make soup or some other fresh foods dinner. These premixed dinners are also healthy alternatives to processed foods, such as salt-laden noodle soup bricks or soup-in-a-cup meals you might otherwise resort to eating.

Ingredients you can layer in jars for different meal or meal-starter combinations include dried pasta, rice, dried vegetables, herbs, and spices—even dried meats—for dinners and sides such as split-pea soup, potato biscuits, or even chocolate truffle pound cake! Think about some of your favorite one-dish meals and consider whether the ingredients could be dried and combined for later use. There are also a growing number of cookbooks and websites devoted to dinner-in-a-jar meals.

TIP 385: *Soak dried beans to reduce cooking time*

Soaking beans reduces cooking time and helps to reduce indigestible sugars that can cause gas. Soak dried beans overnight (about 8–12 hours) in water. For a faster soak, bring beans to a boil in a generous pot of water (about 5 cups of water for each cup of beans) and boil for 2–3 minutes. Reduce the heat and let them stand for 2–4 hours before cooking. Small beans, such as lentils, do not need to be soaked.

TIP 386: *Finally learn what sugar plums are all about!*

Admit it. You've heard of sugar plum fairies from that dance in the *Nutcracker* ballet and "visions of sugar plums" from the poem "'Twas the Night Before Christmas." But have you ever had a sugar plum? There is some debate about what actually constituted a sugar plum back in the days people were dreaming and dancing about them. The common element seemed to be that sugar was used as both a sweetener and a preservative in combination with seeds, fruits, and nuts.

Today, sugar plums are candy confections made from dried dates, cranberries, and prunes mixed with nuts, spices, and sugar. There are a number of recipes for sugar plums readily available through a quick trip to the Internet, whether you're interested in sugar plum recipes that may date as far back as the 16th century or in the 21st-century variety. It's the perfect way to introduce your family to dried fruits and to celebrate the holidays with a new tradition.

FERMENTING

Fermented foods employ microbes to do the work of preserving or transforming the flavor of food. In the process, fermenting preserves—and even creates—nutrients in food, including beneficial bacteria necessary for gut health. As magical as it all sounds, getting started with fermenting requires little more than vegetables, salt, a knife, a cutting board, and a jar. You can start with a simple fermenting project such as sauerkraut. But you may want to experiment with more exotic fermented foods and beverages you won't find at your typical local grocery store, such as kombucha (fermented tea) or kimchi (fermented cabbage).

UNDERSTANDING FERMENTING

TIP 387: Don't be afraid of fermenting

● "Fermenting" sounds so suspicious and unsettling. Is it safe to eat a fermented food? Actually, yes. You eat fermented foods all the time and probably don't even think about it. Sauerkraut, olives, and cheese (and of course wine!) are all fermented. Most preserving methods are designed to stop or slow the growth of microorganisms. In fermentation, microorganisms are encouraged to grow and produce bacteria, molds, or yeasts, which inhibit the growth of other, unwanted microorganisms. Fermented foods are considered live foods because the culturing process continues while the food is in storage.

TIP 388: Fermented foods promote the growth of healthy bacteria in the gut

● The digestive system is like a garden. A garden has plants we want to grow and weeds we need to clear out. In the gut, we have good bacteria we want to nurture and bad bacteria we want to eliminate. The good bacteria perform a multitude of nourishing and supportive functions, including aiding digestion and absorption of vitamins, breaking down ingested toxins, and boosting immunity.

As with a garden, some environmental conditions promote healthy growth while others weaken plants and promote disease. A diet with excessive sugar and refined foods weakens the environment, promoting the overgrowth of harmful organisms, and undermining our health. Including fermented foods in your diet will promote and replenish a healthy bacterial environment in your gut.

TIP 389: *Get familiar with the different types of fermentation*

As you begin to learn about the world of fermented foods, you'll hear a lot of terms that can be confusing. You'll likely hear about wild fermentation, lacto-fermentation, and culturing. It sounds more complicated than it actually is. These are all terms that describe fermentation processes. Wild fermentation occurs spontaneously from the microorganisms that are naturally present on foods. Sauerkraut is an example of wild fermentation because the naturally occurring bacteria on the cabbage are "wild" and have not been introduced. Vegetables are usually fermented through wild fermentation because of the abundance of microorganisms that naturally live on plants.

A wild fermentation can also be a lacto-fermentation, but it doesn't have to be. Lacto-fermentation describes the growth of lactic acid in a fermentation, as when you ferment milk or vegetables.

Culturing is fermentation through the introduction of some sort of microbial starter rather than relying on the "wild" microorganisms in the environment or on the food to do the fermentation. A packet of yeast is a starter or culture for bread, for example. Yogurt is made using a bit of a previous batch of yogurt as a starter. There are other types of starters as well, sometimes called mothers or SCOBY. SCOBY is the acronym for a symbiotic colony of bacteria and yeast—a starter or culture.

TIP 390: Expect a somewhat different result each time you make a fermented foods recipe

🌀 The environment plays a huge role in how a fermentation project turns out. The temperature, the ingredients, the culture or wild microorganisms that will be doing the work, time, and how the ferment is treated during its hours, days, or weeks of fermenting combine to make the final product. It is unlikely that you'll achieve the exact same combination each time you make a fermented foods recipe. Now, that's not to say you can't get consistently good results, because you can. But part of the wonder of fermented foods is that they are living and, as we have all learned by now, living things seem to have minds of their own.

TIP 391: Give foods time to ferment

🌀 If you have embarked on a fermenting project, be prepared to give it plenty of time. Rushing a jar into the refrigerator out of worry that your fermenting project will go bad will only stop the fermentation process since the bacteria that are at work cannot grow and thrive in the cold.

Fruits are naturally high in sugar, which means they will ferment more quickly than vegetables. Most fruits will ferment in about 3–5 days. If you allow fruits to continue fermenting, they will become alcoholic. Let your fruit fermentation keep going and the alcohol will become acetic acid or vinegar. (See? All three phases are good products!) Vegetables take much longer to ferment. Sauerkraut, for example, is fermented for 2–4 weeks or even longer. Some fermented foods are ongoing, with new produce added regularly to make a continuous, fermenting product.

Before you give up because your fermenting project is taking too long, review your recipe and directions and be patient.

FERMENTING EQUIPMENT

TIP 392: *Pick the right container for fermenting*

⚫ There are several factors to consider when selecting the container you'll use for your fermenting project. First, of course, is size. You'll need to pick a container that is large enough to comfortably hold all the ingredients for your ferment. Pick a container that is too large and it will take up space and be difficult to move around. A container with a too-wide diameter will make it difficult to keep your food submerged in the brine and expose too much of the food to the air.

Round containers are easier to work with than square, rectangle, or odd-shaped containers. They allow you to more easily stir the contents. It is also easier to find a round plate or other object to serve as a weight to put on top of the food to keep it submerged. Your container should have a top or you should find some other way to keep it covered during fermentation. This will keep out flies or dust from settling into the food but will also keep out molds or yeasts that could spoil your ferment. Ferments that do not require oxygen or microbes from the air can be fermented in closed jars or containers. The fermentation process produces gases that build up, so you will need to regularly vent jars or provide some mechanism to keep the jar from exploding from the built-up pressure.

TIP 393: *Use a container with an air lock to keep out oxygen*

● Exposure to oxygen can cause problems with fermentation because of the naturally occurring bacteria, molds, and yeasts that are in the air. You can minimize exposure to air by using jars and fermenting buckets fitted with specialized air locks. Available from wine and beer brewing supply stores, the air locks keep air out but allow the gases produced during fermentation to escape so that the container does not break or explode.

TIP 394: *Beware of plastic and metal containers for fermenting*

● Many people use plastic containers for fermenting. However, there is a growing movement of people who are concerned about the use of plastics for foods because of the possibility of chemicals leaching into the food. It is possible that the fermenting process could accelerate chemical leaching. Another concern about plastics is that they are more prone to scratches, where harmful bacteria can hide. If you use plastic, use only food-grade containers for your fermenting project. Garbage cans, plastic household storage bins, or other repurposed containers are not safe for use in preparing fermented foods.

You should avoid using metal for acidic fermenting projects, except for enameled pots or stainless steel. Check carefully to make sure these pots do not have scratches or nicks that will expose the food to the underlayer of metal. Acids can corrode metal and leach the corrosion into the food.

TIP 395: *Test old or antique crocks for lead before using for fermenting*

You can find beautiful old crocks in antiques stores or perhaps you even inherited one that is now living life as an umbrella stand or flower vase. These rustic glazed-ceramic crocks range in size from smaller than a gallon (3.75L) up to an amazing 100 gallons (375L) or more. Many years ago every kitchen had one or more of these crocks and they were used to store butter, flour, sugar—even leftovers. Paraffin was poured over the top when an airtight seal was needed. Crocks were the original Tupperware®!

You can put an antique crock back into service for your fermenting project. But before you do, it's a good idea to test for lead that may have been used in the glazing to avoid the possibility of lead poisoning. Lead paint test kits are inexpensive and do not require a laboratory for processing. You do the test yourself and get the results right away. You can find test kits in the paint department of hardware stores and even some discount stores.

TIP 396: *Invest in a ceramic sauerkraut crock*

You can make sauerkraut in a bowl with a board or plate as a weight. But if you're serious about your sauerkraut and will be making it regularly, you might want to invest in one of the specialized crocks that have fitted, weighted stones that provide consistent pressure to keep the vegetables submerged during the fermentation process. They are available in multiple sizes and make the job much more efficient. Some of these crocks have airtight lids that prevent the formation of unwanted yeasts and molds.

FERMENTING PROCESS

TIP 397: *Pick fresh, tender produce for fermenting*

◉ Pick fresh, mature fruits and vegetables that are free of blemishes, mold, or any signs of decay. Avoid tough or overly mature fruits and vegetables. Overly mature produce will shrivel and decay in the fermenting process. Cucumbers, peppers, and other fruits and vegetables should be free of the waxes and oils used by most grocery stores to extend the display life of produce.

TIP 398: *Some vegetables are better fermenters than others*

◉ One of the reasons you hear so much about sauerkraut is because cabbage is so easy to ferment. Other good fermenters include turnips, radishes, and kohlrabi. Some others vegetables require a bit more attention and work and some vegetables are just downright temperamental. Carrots, onions, and celery mix well with good fermenters but may need a starter if fermented alone. Temperamental fermenters include summer squashes and bell peppers, which can become mushy. Some people consider cucumbers to be temperamental, but don't let that put you off. Take appropriate steps and you can avoid the dreaded hollow pickle syndrome.

Fruits and vegetables with a high sugar content, such as beets and parsnips, can attract yeasts and become more alcoholic than lacto-fermented. It helps to ferment high-sugar foods with lower-sugar foods, such as cabbage and turnips.

TIP 399: *Peel and cut vegetables and fruits into smaller pieces for faster fermenting*

● The smaller the pieces of fruit or vegetables you use, the more surface area there is and the faster your foods will ferment. You can certainly have larger chunks, but with some vegetables, the larger the pieces, the more likely you will be to run into problems. Cabbage is very forgiving, which is why some people ferment nothing but cabbage. But larger cucumbers, turnips, and parsnips, for example, are best sliced, shredded, or cut into matchstick-sized pieces.

If you are making a fermented dish with more than one type of vegetable or fruit, consider how the sizes work together. Cutting pieces to a uniform size will make it more likely that you get a consistent ferment throughout the product. But adding some variety to the sizes and pieces can be a good aesthetic choice.

TIP 400: *Customize your brine*

● Most people are familiar with the traditional brine made of salt and water. A 5 percent basic brine solution can be made with 8 cups (1.9L) of water and 6tbsp of salt. There are other ingredients that can be used to make brines that give different character and flavor to the finished foods. A beer brine can be made from 2 cups (470ml) of basic brine and 2 cups (470ml) of flat beer. Or make a sweet and salty brine from 1 cup of basic brine, ¾ cup (180ml) of apple cider vinegar, 1tbsp of raw honey, and ½tsp of wholegrain Dijon-style mustard. You can even mix brine left over from another batch of food with basic brines to kick start your fermenting project.

TIP 401: Try fermenting in whey

Whey is one of the components of milk and is a by-product of cheese-making. You may have seen whey pooling on the top of yogurt. It's that watery white substance that you probably pour off or mix back in. Whey makes an excellent brine, infusing vegetables with microorganisms that contribute to digestive tract health. A salt brine is often added to the whey brine, which helps keep vegetables crunchy and makes them less susceptible to mold. Although there is not a great amount of lactose in whey, whey brining is not recommended for people who are dairy-intolerant.

If you make your own cheese, you can brine in whey that is left over from cheese-making. Don't worry that you have to make cheese first to get whey though; you can also collect whey from yogurt. Drain plain, active-culture yogurt through a colander double-lined with cheesecloth. Catch the whey in a bowl as it drains. And don't throw away that yogurt when you're done! It makes an excellent spread for English muffins or toast and can be mixed with onions, herbs, spices, or more sweet flavors, such as fruit and honey. There are special yogurt strainers on the market that are handy to have in the kitchen for making yogurt cheese.

TIP 402: *You may need to search for starter cultures to use in fermenting*

● Some fermented foods require the use of starter cultures, special molds, and bacteria that give fermented foods their distinctive taste. It's unlikely that you will find fermenting cultures at your local grocery store, although some Chinese grocery stores and pharmacies do carry koji starter—the culture for making miso. The best place to look is online. Compare reviews to see whether the starters were active and successful.

TIP 403: *Experiment with commercial special vegetable starter cultures*

● There are commercial starters available on the market that can give your ferment a head start, with specialized strains of bacteria that will help your fermented vegetables develop flavor that you couldn't achieve without the starter. It is an easy way to speed up the fermentation process with a known and tested set of bacteria and to get consistent results every time you ferment. These starter cultures are dried bacteria packed in foil envelopes and are available at some health food stores and on the Internet.

TIP 404: *Use canning or pickling salt*

● As with any canning project, use canning or pickling salts. Table salts usually contain anti-caking agents and iodine as additives, which can cloud the brine or cause the food to darken. Salt is an essential ingredient in fermenting foods, so always follow instructions about salt types and measurements precisely.

TIP 405: *Use fresh, whole spices in fermenting*

If your fermenting recipe calls for a whole spice but you only have ground spice in your cabinet, plan on heading to the grocery store. Substituting ground spice for whole can cloud your brine, ruining your fermenting project. Spices can be tied into small muslin bags available at specialty kitchen shops or into cheesecloth tied with kitchen twine. This makes removing the spices a snap at the end of the project.

TIP 406: *You may need to use bottled or filtered water*

Water quality is very important in fermenting projects, both as an ingredient (as with some brines) and for washing produce. Public utility systems routinely treat water with chlorine, which can inhibit the growth of beneficial bacteria in the ferment. Even household well water can be unsuitable. Hard well water has a heavy mineral content that can interfere with acid formation in the fermentation process.

One option is to treat your tap water before using it to reduce mineral content and dissipate chlorine. Boil water for 15 minutes and allow it to sit for 24 hours. Then, gently pour off the water and leave behind the sediment that has precipitated out. Unfortunately, some public utility systems are now using chloramines, a combination of chlorine and ammonia, which cannot be boiled or dissipated out this way. In that case, use distilled or bottled water instead, even for washing and rinsing foods you plan to ferment. Call your public utility water department or visit their website to learn more about what's in your water.

TIP 407: *Keep fermenting foods completely submerged*

⬤ Fermented foods, such as sauerkraut and pickles, should be completely submerged in the brine throughout the fermenting process. Your fermenting container should be fitted with a weight that is placed on top of the food to keep it pushed down into the brine. Some fermenting crocks come equipped with stone weights that fit perfectly into the container. If you are improvising, you can use a plate that is weighted down with a milk jug filled with water. You can also use a food-grade plastic bag filled with a brine solution that will both hold down the food and create a barrier against the air.

If the top of your fermenting food has briefly been exposed to air, it is possible to stir or push it back in and continue with the fermenting project. But if you have ignored your fermenting project for several days and discovered that there is extensive drying, you should call it quits, toss it in the compost bin, and start over.

FERMENTED FOODS

TIP 408: *Get started fermenting with sauerkraut*

⬤ Sauerkraut is nearly synonymous with fermenting. It's no wonder either, since it's so easy to do. Here are the ingredients: fresh cabbage and salt. For equipment, you'll need an airtight jar that you can vent. You can also use a crock and a plate that fits snugly into the jar and something to weigh it down, such as a gallon (3.8L) plastic milk jug filled with water, and a cloth or plastic cover.

Chop or grate the cabbage to the texture you like. You can use the heart or leave it out. Sprinkle with 3–4tbsp of canning salt on the cabbage and mix well. Pack the cabbage/salt mixture into your container by punching it down hard with your fist or a potato masher to remove any air and to begin forcing the moisture out of the cabbage. Seal the jar or cover the mixture with a plate that fits snugly into the crock and place the weight on top and then with the cloth or plastic cover. You want to try to keep out air, so you can also use a food-grade bag filled with salty water over or under the plate to form a more airtight seal.

After a day or two the cabbage should be quite liquid. From time to time, press down the plate to keep the cabbage submerged in the developing brine. If using a jar, vent it very frequently or leave the lid slightly loose so the jar doesn't explode from the gases that will build up. If the sauerkraut seems dry, add some salty water. Keep checking daily. After a few days, begin sampling to see how it tastes. Once you're happy with the result, you can refrigerate your sauerkraut or let it keep fermenting to see what other flavors develop.

TIP 409: *Spice up your sauerkraut*

🌀 You might like to add more complexity to the flavors of your sauerkraut or begin branching out into mixing in other vegetables. Herbs and spices that work well with sauerkraut include dill, mustard and caraway seeds, juniper berries (a little goes a long way), red chili flakes, bay leaves, and garlic. Rather than throwing in the whole kitchen sink, pick one or two additional flavors to begin with and see what appeals to you.

Cabbage combines well with lots of other vegetables for a more colorful kraut. Try red cabbage, napa cabbage, carrots, onions, fennel—even fruits, such as apples, cranberries, and pineapple.

TIP 410: *Make your sauerkraut international*

🌀 There are countless versions of sauerkraut that are unique to many countries and cultures. The most famous, perhaps, is kimchi, the traditional Korean dish. Kimchi often includes napa cabbage, daikon radish or turnips, and carrots, chilies, garlic, and ginger. South American versions may be flavored with mint and cilantro. The American South has a version too— with onions, carrots, apples, green bell pepper, celery seed, dry mustard, and honey. If you have a family culinary heritage, ask older family members if they ever fermented foods and what flavors they used. All things old are new again!

TIP 411: *You can make sauerkraut without salt*

🌀 Alternative methods of fermenting cabbage to make sauerkraut include using wine, seaweed, or a combination of caraway, celery, and dill seeds. Each method has its own unique flavors, but none will keep as long as salt-fermented sauerkraut and they all tend to be less crispy.

TIP 412: *Don't worry about foaming or pink sauerkraut*

⚫ Fermenting foods will often begin to foam a bit, particularly in the early stages of the fermenting process. Don't worry about a little foam. Just skim it off so that you can better monitor the food underneath. Similarly, sometimes sauerkraut may turn a little pink. This is a byproduct of yeasts in action and can occur when the salinity is more than 3 percent. It is not harmful, so don't worry.

TIP 413: *Serve up your sauerkraut*

⚫ Most of us know sauerkraut as a hot dog topping, even if we only watched the grownups eat their hot dogs that way. There's also the Reuben sandwich, made with sauerkraut, corned beef, Swiss cheese, and Thousand Island dressing on rye bread. The beauty of these two classics is that the sauerkraut is not cooked, which preserves all those lovely little microorganisms that are good for the gut.

There are also the sauerkraut versions of comfort food: sauerkraut meatballs, sauerkraut meatloaf, sauerkraut casserole, and who can forget sauerkraut pizza! But sauerkraut can be quite upscale. Some sushi restaurants use sauerkraut in nori rolls. In France, a wintertime family dinner might be *choucroute garnie*, a deliciously spiced dish from the Alsatian region that combines sauerkraut with sausages and other salted meats and potatoes. Paula Deen makes an American South version of the same dish with babyback ribs, potatoes, and sauerkraut. You can make sauerkraut dumplings, sauerkraut pancakes, sauerkraut soup, and sauerkraut burgers. Well, you get the idea.

TIP 414: *Know the difference between fermented and fresh-pack pickles*

In general, there are two ways to make pickles. The pickles you can buy in the grocery store are almost always fresh-pack pickles. Fresh-pack pickles are made by briefly curing the cucumbers or other produce in a salty brine and then packing them with vinegar before processing in the canner. Fermented pickles, on the other hand, are made in a crock or barrel. They are covered in a salty brine and left to cure at room temperature for 4–6 weeks. During that time bacteria work to produce lactic acid, which keeps the produce from rotting, but also gives it that distinct pickled flavor. A hybrid version of the fermented pickle is the refrigerated pickle, in which the cucumbers are fermented for a week and then put right into the refrigerator without processing. They must be used within a few weeks.

TIP 415: Spot problems with fermentation

🌀 Sometimes, things go wrong. There are a lot of forces working in concert in any fermenting project—the container, the temperature, the naturally occurring bacteria in the environment, the condition of the food and other ingredients, and, of course, time. If you ferment enough foods, you're bound to have a batch that putrefies or molds.

Other signs of problems are slimy films or fuzzy mold growth. Some websites and books will tell you to remove mold if there is only a small amount and to keep fermenting and checking daily. However, it's best to be on the safe side and throw out any food with mold since there can be mold spores throughout the food that you can't see. Plenty of people would loudly disagree with wasting such lovely food, and you may decide to make your own informed decision about how to deal with small amounts of mold.

Foods that smell bad or of alcohol (unless they are supposed to smell like alcohol) should also be thrown out. Needless to say, if you see maggots, you won't want to eat that food. Throw it out. No one will disagree with you. And always keep your fermenting foods covered to keep out pests.

TIP 416: *Try other fermented foods*

⚫ Is the purpose of fermenting foods to presere them or to add flavor? Surely some fermented foods store quite well. But many of the most popular fermented foods are made that way because of the distinctive flavors fermenting creates rather than for long-term preservation. Yogurt is fermented and yet we know it must be refrigerated after fermentation and used within a short period of time. The same is true of soft cheeses, buttermilk, and kefir, the fermented drink made from milk and kefir grains. We don't need to debate the philosophical reasons for fermenting to feel comfortable recommending that you explore making more healthy fermented foods at home, whether you can store them for months or not.

The obvious fermented foods to try are yogurt and soft, spreadable cheeses, such as crème fraîche or Neufchâtel. Making fermented beverages such as wine, beer, cider, and mead is becominga popular hobby, even with retail storefront locations selling supplies. But there is a whole other world of fermented foods that is worth exploring. Kombucha is a fermented tea made using a SCOBY (symbiotic colony of bacteria and yeast). You will need to find someone willing to share their SCOBY or purchase a SCOBY over the Internet to get started making this curious drink. Many breads are fermented, with sourdough bread being the most widely known. But the spongy Ethiopian injera bread is also fermented. International foods offer a cornucopia of fermenting options, including miso, tempeh, tofu, and poi.

TIP 417: *Find a place to sample fermented foods*

⚫ Before investing in special equipment, starter cultures, or grains of a new food for fermenting, visit a restaurant that serves it and see how you like it. You'll not only be able to evaluate if you consider it worth the effort, you'll get to sample how the food should taste.

SALT CURING
AND SMOKING

Salt curing is the process of adding flavor to and preserving food, which can then be smoked—or not. You can cure and smoke beef, pork, poultry, fish, and wild game, as well as nuts and cheese. Our ancestors used salt curing and smoking because fresh meat wasn't always as close as the local grocery store. Today, adding flavor and having more control over how our foods are prepared are some of the top reasons for preserving meats this way. The opportunity to get outdoors is an important motivation for some cooks. These tips will introduce you to salt curing and smoking as a way to preserve foods at home.

CURING AND SMOKING BASICS

TIP 418: *Know the keys to safe and successful salting and curing*

There are four keys to safe and successful salting and curing: good sanitation and handling practices; fresh, quality meats; strict attention to temperature control; and the right salt content.

Any food preserving project that involves meat requires careful attention to sanitation and proper handling practices, including washing of equipment, tools, and hands in hot, soapy water, avoiding cross-contamination with other foods, and proper handling of the meat before, during, and after preparation. Any slips along the way could introduce bacteria that is both unsafe and could promote spoilage.

Use only the freshest and best-quality meats that you can find. Don't try to cure any meats that have been frozen because changes in texture occur during freezing and can impact the curing process. As with canning and drying meats, know the source and handling practices to ensure that you aren't getting a product that has been kept above a safe temperature or otherwise handled without the best sanitary standards.

Maintaining a steady temperature is one of the biggest challenges in salting and curing at home. Meat for salting and curing must be kept as near as possible at a temperature of 38°F (3°C). Much colder and it will be difficult for the salt to penetrate into the meat tissues. Any warmer and you increase the chances of spoilage.

TIP 419: *Understand brine curing*

Brine curing, also called wet curing, is the process of soaking the meat or fish in a liquid brine solution for 24–48 hours at a temperature of 36–40°F (2–4°C). Because of the temperature, brine curing is usually done in the refrigerator.

The formula for the brine solution will depend on the type of meat, how it is cut, and how long you plan to leave the meat unrefrigerated after preserving. A basic brine can be prepared from water, canning salt, and sugar, if desired. The brine strength depends on the type of meat. Brines should be chilled before using and regularly replaced during the brining process if your cut of meat is large. It's also a good idea to turn the meat over once or twice a day during the brining period. Never reuse a brine solution.

TIP 420: *It is best to go with a premixed preparation when using nitrates and nitrites in curing*

⬤ Our ancestors used potassium nitrate, also known as saltpeter, in the curing of meats. Although some recipes call for the use of saltpeter, today we mostly use sodium nitrite alone or in combination with nitrate. The purpose is the same—to create flavor and extend the storage life of meats by protecting against harmful microorganisms and rancidity. Using nitrates or nitrites also gives meat a red or pink color. Meats brined without nitrates or nitrites can be grayish in color.

The National Center for Home Food Preservation (NCHFP) cautions that adding nitrate or nitrite to meat must be done with extreme caution since these substances can be toxic to humans in the wrong amount. In commercial foods, federal regulations permit a maximum addition of 2.75oz (78g) of sodium or potassium nitrate per 100lb (45.36kg) of chopped meat, and 0.25oz (7g) sodium or potassium nitrite per 100lb (45.35kg) of chopped meat. Since the home preserver will probably be preserving in quantities of much less than 100lb, this type of precise measuring becomes very difficult. That is why the NCHFP recommends using commercially prepared brining mixes for home curing. These premixes include salt along with the nitrates or nitrites in precise amounts. Some also include spices and simulated hickory smoke flavorings. You can find these mixes at some grocery stores and online.

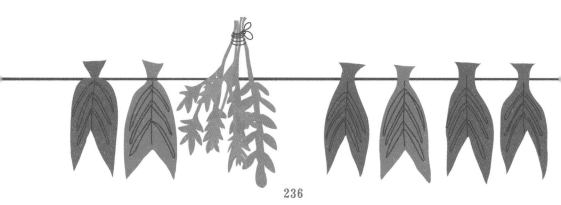

TIP 421: *Inject large cuts of meat with the brine*

Large cuts of meat take longer to brine than smaller cuts. In order for the brine to penetrate into the thicker parts of the meat, use a brine pump, which looks like a large syringe, to inject the brine deep into the meat.

TIP 422: *Understand dry curing*

In dry curing, the cure mix is applied directly to the meat rather than submerging the meat in the brine or curing solution. Dry curing is best used for sausages, bacon, and hams that will be air-dried. Methods for applying the dry cure differ. One method is to rub the cure on the meat so that it is covered. Another method is to apply the cure repeatedly over the curing period.

After the dry cure is applied, the meat is covered, sealed, and kept at 36–40°F (2–4°C), usually in the refrigerator, while the curing takes place. The meat should be placed in a drying box or covered and placed on a tray fitted with a rack to allow the moisture that is drawn from the meat to drip below so that the meat is not sitting in it.

The length of time for a dry cure depends on the meat and the effect you are trying to achieve. After curing, the curing mixture is rinsed to remove the cure mix and is then air-dried or cold-smoked.

TIP 423: *Understand combination curing*

⚫ As the name suggests, combination curing is a mix between curing types—rubbing with a dry cure and injecting the meat with a brine cure. Combination curing reduces the overall curing time and reduces the risk of spoilage because the curing agents are applied both inside and outside the meat.

TIP 424: *Cold smoking is used to dry cure meat and add flavor*

⚫ Cold smoking, sometimes called dry smoking, does not preserve meat. Rather, cold smoking is used to add flavor to foods and also to dry cured meats before storing. Cold-smoked foods are held at 80°F (27°C) or lower while surrounding them with smoke, which requires a special setup and equipment to keep foods away from the fire used to create the smoke. Cured and smoked bacon and smoked salmon are good examples of the results of this process. Because of the relatively low temperature used in cold smoking, other foods can also be smoked this way, including cheese, butter, nuts, and eggs.

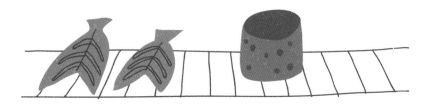

TIP 425: *Be aware of the warnings related to cold smoking meats*

There are many sources, including those of the National Center for Home Food Preservation, that caution against cold smoking at home because of the dangers associated with processing meats at temperatures in the so-called danger zone (40–140°F [4–60°C]) and the difficulty of maintaining the correct environment in a non-commercial atmosphere. Strict attention to the process and control of the variables using the proper equipment can address these areas of concern.

In addition, because cold smoking does not preserve the meat, it should only be used for meats that have been fermented, salted, or cured. Most cold-smoked products must be cooked to an internal temperature of 160°F (70°C) to be safe. Smoked salmon is a notable exception. If you are giving your cured and smoked meat as a gift, make sure the lucky recipient understands it must still be cooked to be safe.

TIP 426: *Cold smoking can take a great deal of time*

Cold smoking cheese can be done in as little as an hour, but cold-smoking meats can be a lengthy process. Bacon, salami, and fish can take 4–8 hours to smoke. A ham can take 24–48 hours or more! But the amount of smoking time is highly variable and depends very much on the effect you are trying to achieve.

TIP 427: *You can smoke your meat—or not*

Cold smoking is the method of adding the smoked flavor to foods after curing and to dry the surface of the meat. Smoking by itself is not a method of preserving food.

TIP 428: Don't confuse cold smoking with hot smoking

Cold smoking and hot smoking are very different processes with different purposes. Hot smoking, such as large pig barbecues, is really a slow-cook method of preparing food.

TIP 429: Liquid smoke is not smoke

It probably doesn't surprise you that the smoky flavor added to chips, sauces, and other processed foods isn't achieved through direct smoking. A smoke flavor is added to the recipe. If that smoked taste appeals to you and you don't want to go the cold or hot smoker route, you can still achieve the smoke flavor with liquid smoke.

Liquid smoke is made from capturing the smoke from burning sawdust in water or oil. It comes in a bottle and is available in the condiments section of the grocery store. You should know, however, that smoke contains cancer-causing chemicals, some of which may be captured in products such as liquid smoke.

TIP 430: Avoid smoking meat in the summer

Unless you have a specialized smoker that can keep temperatures in a safe range—around 80°F (27°C)—it is best to limit your meat-smoking activities to times of the year when you can reasonably expect temperatures to be more mild. Even though the fire that produces the smoke for cold smoking is held away from the meat storage area, temperatures in an enclosed smoke house or smoke box can reach unsafe levels that will permit bacteria to grow and spoil the meat.

EQUIPMENT AND SUPPLIES

TIP 431: *Make sure the container you plan to use for brining is large enough*

● Crocks, bowls, and jars are all suitable containers for brining as long as they are large enough to completely submerge the meat in the brine solution. If you use plastic, make sure it is food-grade plastic and not a repurposed container, such as a garbage can. Plastic can leach chemicals into the brine and into the meat. As with canning, metal bowls or barrels should be of a non-reactive metal, such as stainless steel. A stone or plate weighted with a water-filled milk jug may be needed to weight the meat and hold it under the solution.

TIP 432: *Pick the right smoker for your needs*

● Choosing the right smoker will take some research since they come in a vast array of sizes, styles, and fuel types. Some sell for as little as $50 while others go for thousands of dollars. It helps to have a clear idea of what and how you want to smoke. If you don't, it's best to start with an inexpensive smoker and upgrade your equipment as you learn and gain experience. For preserving you will want a smoker that does cold smoking, so don't confuse products that only do hot smoking or hot smoking and grilling.

Charcoal, wood pellets, wood, gas, and electricity can all be used as fuel. Charcoal and wood-burning products add their own special flavors to the food, but unless you get a smoker that self-loads, which will be more expensive, you will need to be able to spend the time to feed and monitor the fire during smoking. Electric and gas smokers, although pricier, are simpler and make it easier to maintain an even temperature.

TIP 433: *You can build your own cold smoker*

If you are fairly handy with tools you can build your own home cold smoker system. There are basically four parts to a cold smoker: a place for the fire; a box or shed to enclose the food; hooks and shelves to hold the food during smoking; and a system for venting smoke into the food storage area. The distance between the fire and the food storage area doesn't have to be very far, but it does need to be far enough to protect the food from the heat.

If you have visited historic homes, you probably saw smoke houses that were whole outbuildings devoted to smoking and storing meats. Your system doesn't have to be so grand to be effective, particularly since it is unlikely you'll need to cure and smoke all the meat you'll need or want to get through several months, like our colonial ancestors did. But you can use an old shed or even an old refrigerator. You can use a metal drum if you know how it was used and are sure that it is clean and chemical-free. There are plans for building your own cold smoker setup in books and on the Internet.

TIP 434: *Use a handheld, portable smoker for small, fast smoking projects*

If your smoking ambitions only extend to giving a touch of smoke to a cheese or other product, a handheld, portable model might be all that you need. They are sold with different types of sawdust for different flavors, such as hickory and apple wood.

TIP 435: *Source your wood carefully*

🔆 You must be careful about the source of your wood. Wood salvaged from building sites could well have been treated with chemicals that will render your foods inedible and even dangerous. Wood from pruning or that is sold for fireplaces might be okay, but you will do even better to source your own wood so you know where it was from.

The best time to collect wood is in the fall or winter before the sap rises in the spring, adding moisture and a bitter taste to the wood. If your wood was cut with a chainsaw, make sure that any oil residue from the saw is removed or you'll end up with an unpleasant-smelling smoke. You will need to convert your wood to sawdust or shavings to make smoke, depending on the smoker type. Always follow manufacturer instructions for wood preparation. An electric planer connected to a shop vacuum works well to collect the shavings. Once your shavings are prepared, seal them in a plastic bag to retain moisture until you're ready to smoke.

TIP 436: *Experiment with different types of woods for different flavors*

⚫ Different types of wood imbue different flavors to your smoked foods. The best types of wood are a matter of opinion. You have probably tried hickory-smoked or apple-smoked meats at some time. Apricot and cherry woods give a sweetish, fruity flavor to the food. Almond imbues the food with a nutty and sweet flavor. Wood from a lilac has a vaguely floral flavor. Experiment with different wood types to achieve different characteristics in your final product.

TIP 437: *You must have proper humidity during smoking*

⚫ Cold smoking should be done at 50 percent to 85 percent humidity, depending on the food being smoked. Of course, the humidity of the geographic area and the time of year play a role in humidity. There are a couple of things that you can do to raise the humidity to the recommended level in your cold smoker. You can use moist wood chips or sawdust to create the smoke. You can also put pans of water in the smoker, which will evaporate and raise the humidity level. Other, less comfortable options for the person minding the smoke house include smoking at night, when humidity is higher, or during rainy weather.

CURED AND SMOKED FOODS

TIP 438: *Take care in adjusting the salinity of your brine*

Having the correct amount of salt in the brine is essential because it is the salt that works to preserve the food. It is for that reason that care must be taken when adjusting the salinity of the brine. Reducing the salinity to below safe levels can allow bacteria to grow. A 5 percent salt solution can inhibit the growth of *Salmonella* but still allow other types of bacteria, including *Staphylococcus* or *Listeria monocytogenes*, to grow. A 15 to 20 percent salt solution made of 1lb (450g) of salt to 4 pints of water or liquid will prevent the growth of salt-tolerant bacteria.

It is best to carefully follow a proven recipe from a knowledgeable source for your brine solution. If you want to adjust your own brine, you can use a hydrometer to measure the salinity. Available from science supply and wine and beer brewing companies, a hydrometer is a fairly simple tool to use if you follow the calculations carefully.

TIP 439: *Add flavors to your brine*

The brine is extremely important in curing meat because, as the salt draws the moisture out of the meat, the flavors from the brine are infused into the meat. When you mix your own brine, you get to customize it—and thus the meat—with the flavors you like. You can use garlic, bay leaves, cloves, juniper berries, thyme, rosemary, coriander, ginger, black peppercorns—whatever you like.

TIP 440: *Stop over-worrying about nitrites*

In the 1970s, news stories were filled with warnings and scares about the use of potentially carcinogenic nitrites in bacon, hot dogs, and other processed meats. You will still see foods that boast being nitrite-free—probably to appeal to those of us who remember the 1970s. But to quote the American Medical Association, while large quantities of nitrites can cause serious damage, "given the current FDA and USDA regulations on the use of nitrites, the risk of developing cancer as a result of consumption of nitrites-containing food is negligible."

TIP 441: *Know about Prague powders or pink powders*

⬤ Prague powders, sometimes called pink powders or pink salts, are specially formulated premix curing salts that come in two formulations. Prague powder #1 includes 93.75 percent table salt and 6.25 percent sodium nitrite and is used in making sausages and corned beef. Prague powder #2 contains sodium nitrate in addition to sodium nitrite and is used in making dry-cured meats like hard salami, pepperoni, and prosciutto. Because they include nitrites and nitrates, the pink coloring in Prague powders is added so that it won't be mistaken for ordinary salt.

TIP 442: *Use a grinder to prepare meat for sausages*

⬤ Meat for sausage must be properly ground to allow the spices and other flavors to be evenly distributed in the mix. A grinder with a fine grind is really the only method to get the consistency you'll want. If your meat is particularly gristly, you may need to grind it twice—once at a regular grind and the second time with a finer grinding plate.

TIP 443: *Brine corned beef for St. Patrick's Day*

The corned beef traditionally eaten on St. Patrick's Day isn't an Irish tradition, but rather one that originated in the Irish-American celebration of the holiday. It's quite easy to make at home, doesn't require cold smoking, and beats anything you can buy in a can. So why not give it a try?

There is actually no corn in corned beef. The "corn" refers to corns of salt—a salt brine. Corned beef usually uses the tougher cuts of beef with plenty of fat. Brisket is the traditional choice, but you can also use a flat cut for a leaner dish. If you use a commercial preparation with nitrates for the basic brine your meat will retain its distinctive red color. But it isn't necessary from a safety standpoint.

Begin your brine a week or more before you plan to cook. After mixing your brine solution, immerse the meat and cover, placing it in the coldest part of your refrigerator. Better yet is to brine it in a spare refrigerator to reduce any temperature fluctuations from the opening and closing of the door. After brining, rinse and pat dry. Roast or boil the beef immersed in water and with carrots, onion, and celery. Cooking may take 3–4 hours, depending on the size of the meat. It is done when you can easily cut it with a sharp knife.

You can make a deli-style corned beef, excellent for slicing onto sandwiches, using a dry rub premix.

TIP 444: *You can make home-cured salt cod in about a week*

⚫ Salt cod is less widely known in the United States than in other countries, where it is a regular ingredient in foods from everyday dishes to holiday feasts. The French comfort food *brandade de morue*, or creamed salt cod, and *baccalà*, the traditional Italian Christmas Eve dish, are just two of the dishes you can make with your own salt cod supply.

Making salt cod is fairly easy. You will start off with a fresh cod fillet, a rather large slab of fish. Wash and dry the fillet and then rub it thoroughly with canning salt. Make sure to massage the salt into every small crevice of the fish. Next, pack the fish into more salt and wrap it all in muslin or cheesecloth so it looks like a little mummy. Use kitchen twine to secure the bundle. Place the fish on a wire rack in the refrigerator to allow for air circulation. After 24 hours, unwrap and rinse the fish in cold water. Rewrap the fish in clean muslin or cheesecloth and place it in a dish in the refrigerator. For about a week you will need to turn the fish and discard any accumulated liquid. You can store the salt cod in the refrigerator for up to 9 months.

Allow plenty of time to prepare your salt cod before use. You will need to rehydrate the cod by soaking it in cold water for a couple of days. Regularly change the soaking water to remove all the excess salt.

TIP 445: *Rinse meats before cooking to reduce salt*

🐷 Cured meats may be more salty than you like. You can decrease the saltiness by rinsing, soaking, or even partially boiling the meat before using it in your recipe. When soaking, replace the water with fresh water a couple of times. Remember though, not to allow the meat to rise to 40°F (4°C) or higher for 2 hours or more. If you plan to give the meat a lengthy soak, do it in the refrigerator.

TIP 446: *Take steps to prevent bitter- or dirty-tasting smoked meats*

🐷 Meats that have been oversmoked can taste unpleasantly bitter or even dirty. Other causes of bitter-tasting meat include meats touching during smoking, using green wood, and improper use of intake and exhaust vents to control airflow. Closing the vents traps the smoke inside the smoker and stops the airflow. Cold, trapped smoke will go stale and will cause a bitter, acrid taste. Carefully monitor vents to ensure proper airflow.

TIP 447: *Avoid hard, dry smoked meats and soggy meats*

🐷 Meats that are hard and dry may have been brined too long or in too strong a brining solution. Excessive smoking or higher than recommended temperatures can also contribute to less tender and moist meats. Meats that are soggy may have been in a too weak brine, which will require a longer smoking time, negatively affecting taste.

TIP 448: *Try making home-smoked nuts*

● Smoked nuts available in stores are usually artificially flavored. You can smoke almonds, chestnuts, pumpkin, and sunflower seeds in the cold smoker. Nuts should be shelled and skins removed before smoking. You can easily remove skins, as on almonds, by quickly blanching and peeling.

To salt nuts and seeds before smoking, soak them in a concentrated brine solution for 6–10 hours. Spread nuts or seeds on a rack or tray and cold smoke for 1–4 hours.

TIP 449: *You can smoke cheese at home*

● Home-smoked cheeses will last longer than those that aren't smoked. Try cold-smoking cheeses such as Swiss, Edam, cheddar, or provolone. Always keep the smoker cool—about 70°F (20°C). Prepare the cheeses by removing any packaging and wax coverings. Cut cheese into slices no more than 2in (5cm) thick. Smoke lightly for about 1–4 hours.

COLD STORAGE/
ROOT CELLARING

Root cellaring doesn't have to involve roots—or even a cellar! It is another term for cold storage and can be accomplished in garages, on porches, and even right in the garden. You can preserve and store vast quantities of unprocessed foods from your garden, pick-your-own farm, or farmers' market and save money, conserve energy, and have a ready supply of healthy foods year-round. These tips will get you started and expand your preserving repertoire.

GETTING STARTED WITH COLD STORAGE

TIP 450: *Consider root cellaring or cold storage*

⬤ Just the sound of the words "root cellar" conjures up visions of old, windswept farms, squeaky wooden doors with iron latches, and the smell of damp earth. Surely this isn't a modern way to preserve food! It's true that root cellars were how our ancestors would keep foods through the long winter months before the age of refrigeration. But the concept behind a root cellar—cold storage—is as valid today as it was when our great grandparents used them.

A root cellar is any place you can store foods using the natural cooling and insulating effects of the earth. Root cellars work by keeping foods cool and moist. The cool temperatures slow the release of ethylene gas and the growth of microorganisms that cause foods to decay. We all know what a potato looks like when it spoils and dries out. Moisture from the earth keeps foods from drying out and spoiling.

A root cellar can be set up in a basement, in an outbuilding dug fully or partially into the ground, or even in containers, such as metal garbage cans or barrels, buried in the ground with the top exposed. Even if a root cellar is out of the question, you can still create suitable cold storage areas in dark, cool spaces around your home. Space can be found under stairs, in basements, in attics, in unheated rooms—in all sorts of nooks and crannies!

TIP 451: *Use cold storage to extend the season for local foods*

⬤ People have all sorts of motivations for preserving foods. One of the benefits of—and a growing reason for—using cold storage is to extend the timeframe in which you can eat locally grown foods. The local foods movement has made a compelling case for eating more foods grown close to where we live. "Eating local," as it is often called, reduces the carbon footprint of our food choices by reducing the energy required to package and move food long distances for consumption. It is also a way of supporting local farmers who struggle to compete against big agricultural companies. In addition, eating locally grown foods helps to preserve the diverse varieties of fruits and vegetables, including heirloom varieties, which would never be offered by large commercial growers because they do not tolerate the harvesting, packaging, and storage methods required for long-distance shipping.

The challenge with eating local foods year-round is that most of us don't live in places where food can grow year-round. Even using cold storage you may not be able to eat a locally grown cantaloupe or tomato in March. But with appropriate storage, you can keep and eat some foods for weeks and even months after the harvest.

TIP 452: Create a cold storage area in your basement

● The optimal temperature range for cold storage is 32–38°F (0–3°C). That is much cooler than the average household basement stays 12 months out of the year. You can create an environment that approximates that as closely as possible by partitioning off a basement corner. The best choice is a northeast or northwest corner. Build walls and a ceiling with good insulation. Take care to plug holes to exclude mice looking for a winter banquet. Provide adequate ventilation to keep too much moisture from building up in a small space.

Think through what kinds of foods you plan to store and build shelves or bins and collect baskets, pallets, and containers to hold the produce. As you can probably tell, your cold storage area should be larger than a closet if you want to try to feed your family on local foods well into the winter. An 8–10ft (2.4–3m) square space is a good size. There are very good plans available free of charge on the Internet.

TIP 453: Create a mini root cellar with a barrel or garbage can

● You can harness the insulating powers of the earth without having to build a whole structure. A buried barrel or garbage can dug into the earth with the top exposed for access will work quite well. Access will be easier if you bury the barrel at an angle and mound soil over the shallower end. Fill the barrel with vegetables tucked into straw, hay, or moss to insulate and cushion them. Top off the packing with a good layer of whatever packing material you're using to protect vegetables closest to the lid. Cover the whole assemblage with a board or lid, making sure you clamp it on tight to protect against burrowing critters and the elements.

TIP 454: *Repurpose an old refrigerator to make a root cellar*

🌑 A nonworking refrigerator can be given new life as a root cellar when buried in the ground. Remove the motor, shelves, and drawers as well as removing any fluids that could potentially leak. Research and observe any safety precautions for these fluids, particularly if the refrigerator is one of the older models that used CFCs for cooling. Disable any locking mechanisms so the door can't become accidentally stuck closed. Dig a hole with dimensions 1ft (30cm) larger than the refrigerator. Position the refrigerator on its back in the hole so that the door is just above ground level. Evaluate the contours and slope of your land carefully to make sure that rainwater flow can't seep in and ruin your stored food.

TIP 455: *Look around your house for nooks and crannies to store foods*

🌑 Enclosed porches, an unheated utility room, or even rooms in the house you can shut off from the heating system can also make good storage areas to overwinter produce in baskets and boxes. Even if these spaces don't qualify as ideal, they can help extend the storage time of produce you want to keep.

Evaluate the space by monitoring a thermometer in the area. Cold is good, but freezing is not good. If the space gets below freezing you can still use it, but you'll need to remember to move produce to a warmer area—at least temporarily—when temperatures drop below freezing.

TIP 456: *Different vegetables and fruits require different storage conditions*

◉ It would be grand if a one-size-fits-all space could serve the long-term storage requirements for all fruits and vegetables. But the fact is that some produce needs warmer conditions and some cooler. Some produce needs moist conditions and some dry. Fruits and vegetables fall into one of four categories: cold/moist, cool/moist, cold/dry, and warm/dry. Cold is generally 32–36°F (0–3°C), cool is more in the range of 40–50°F (4–10°C), and warm is 50–60°F (10–16°C). Moist is humidity of 90–95 percent and dry is humidity between 65 and 80 percent.

Fruits and vegetables that require cold/moist conditions include apples, Brussels sprouts, cabbages, carrots, cauliflower, celery, corn, grapes, leeks, parsnips, pears, radishes, and rutabagas. Produce that requires cool/moist conditions generally are stored for a shorter timeframe and include eggplant, cantaloupe, watermelon, and sweet peppers. Garlic and onions need cool/dry conditions. Produce that needs warm/dry conditions include pumpkins, winter squash, and sweet potatoes.

TIP 457: *Pack produce to help achieve optimal storage conditions*

⬤ Produce packing materials perform several functions: moisture retention, insulation from fluctuating temperatures, and reduction of disease transmission. Vegetables that prefer a more moist environment should never be left exposed directly to air. They benefit from being packed in moistened sand, sawdust, or peat moss. Plastic bags can be used to line baskets and boxes containing these vegetables, but they should be perforated to prevent condensation, which will rot produce.

TIP 458: *Use a minimum/maximum hygro-thermometer to track temperatures*

⬤ You can best evaluate the environment you're using or considering for cold storage by monitoring temperatures using a minimum/maximum hygro-thermometer. These specialized thermometers record the highest daily minimum and maximum temperature as well as humidity. They easily reset with the touch of a button. You can find inexpensive versions of these thermometers at hardware stores and online that record temperatures as low as −20°F (−29°C) and as high as 120°F (49°C).

TIP 459: *Keep shelves away from walls and containers off of floors*

⬤ Placing storage shelves flush against the wall reduces air circulation and can promote mold growth. The same is true for storage bins placed directly on the floor. Move shelves away from walls a few inches and lift baskets and crates off the floor with pallets or bricks.

TIP 460: Take steps to raise the humidity in your root cellar or cold storage area

The optimal humidity conditions for cold storage are much higher than naturally occur in the average house—even in the basement. You will probably need to take steps to increase the humidity. If you have a root cellar with a packed soil floor and need to raise the humidity, you can spread a layer of gravel on the floor and regularly sprinkle it with water. Alternatively, you could place buckets or shallow pans of water in your storage area. Check them regularly to refill so the humidity level doesn't drop. If your storage area is exceptionally dry, you may need to invest in a cool air humidifier, which will need to be monitored and refilled regularly.

TIP 461: Keep out the light

If your cold storage area has windows, cover them with cardboard or install shades that can be kept closed. Light can encourage vegetables to sprout and grow and will hasten the deterioration of stored foods.

TIP 462: *Keep out the pests*

⬤ Pests can do an amazing amount of damage to stored produce before you even know it. Unless you like the idea of sharing your root cellar hoardings with rodents and pantry pests, you'll need to take steps to make sure they don't get the chance. The first line of defense is a good offense. Take care to rid produce of hitchhikers that can ride in on vegetables from the garden. Promptly remove any produce that shows signs of wormholes or other insect damage.

You may not notice any sign of mice or voles in the summer months, but those critters begin their migration to warmer quarters when the weather changes in the fall. Rodents seem to think that houses are grand places to spend the winter months. It takes perseverance to identify and block all the nooks and crannies a mouse can slip through. Use hardware wire, wood, and nails, since mice can eat through aluminum foil or spray foams used to plug up holes.

TIP 463: *Get professional help with pests if you need it*

⬤ If mice are tucking into your vegetable supply and all your attempts to stop the marauding invaders fail, you may want to consider enlisting the help of a commercial exterminator. Search for someone who specializes in "pest exclusion." Until you figure out how the critters are slipping in, set traps. There are very effective live traps that will allow you to catch critters and relocate them to a more suitable location without feeling particularly guilty about it.

TIP 464: *Give your root cellar a spring cleaning*

Even the best-maintained root cellar will need a thorough annual cleaning and inspection. The best time for this chore is in the spring, when most of the stored produce from the previous season has been used. Empty the storage area of all contents, then sweep and vacuum to remove all dust and debris on floors, shelves, and spiderwebs that are hiding in corners. Clean vents and air out the root cellar for a couple of days. This is also the time to repair shelves and inventory baskets and other containers so you can begin collecting what you need for the new harvest season.

TIP 465: *Try leaving some vegetables right in the ground for storage*

Some root vegetables, such as carrots, parsnips, Jerusalem artichokes, and turnips, can remain right in the ground during the cold winter months until you're ready to use them. Depending on the weather where you live, you may need to mulch heavily—as much as 18in (45cm)—and cover the mulch with cardboard or other porous material secured with landscaping pins to keep it from blowing away. Mark rows with string so you know where to begin digging.

TIP 466: *Use a cold frame to keep cool-weather vegetables growing*

A cold frame is a bottomless box that sits on the ground over your vegetables. It has a window that hinges open and closed to allow you access to the vegetables and a frame that is slanted so that the back is higher than the front. A cold frame is best positioned so that it faces south to catch the rays of the winter sun. Cool-weather vegetables can continue to grow in a cold frame well into the winter. Vegetables suited to growing this way include lettuce, spinach, arugula, carrots, leeks, and scallions.

TIP 467: *Build a hoop tunnel to grow salad greens*

Another way to extend the growing season for your salad greens well into fall and even winter is with a hoop tunnel. A hoop tunnel is like a small do-it-yourself greenhouse. You can build one over your vegetables using concrete wire, PVC tubing, or other material to create the frame and using heavy-grade plastic for the cover. You'll need to secure the edges with bricks, boards, or landscape pins to avoid having your hoop tunnel turn into a sail with the first big wind.

TIP 468: *Build a hay bale fortress to extend the life of other garden plants*

Vegetables that are too big to fit in a cold frame can be given a reprieve from the ravages of winter with a hay bale fortress. Stack hay bales to completely surround the vegetables you want to protect. Fashion a cover from an old storm window or other materials that will allow light to reach the plants. If weather is very cold, you can pile on old rugs or blankets to help hold in the heat. Your vegetables may not make it through the whole winter, but you can extend the time frame for harvest.

TIP 469: *Create small, portable cold storage containers*

🍎 Don't despair if a root cellar or outbuilding is out of the question or just out of the budget. You can create portable cold storage using coolers, large plastic or galvanized tubs, or plain cardboard boxes. Layer vegetables such as carrots with sand, making sure to fill all the nooks and crannies around the veggies. Spray the sand with water to raise the moisture level. Wrap apples and peaches in newspaper and layer gently into cardboard boxes. Depending on your situation, you may need to move these portable storage solutions around to keep the temperature right.

TIP 470: *Start collecting cold storage materials*

🍎 The best packing or layering material for cold storage varies for each fruit or vegetable, depending on how tender the produce is and how much moisture and air circulation it needs to stay in good condition during storage. While you are evaluating and preparing your root cellar or cold storage area, begin collecting items that could be useful as packing material. Newspapers, wood shavings, peat moss, sand (not from the beach), mesh bags, egg cartons, old pantyhose, and cardboard boxes are all useful for cold storage packing. An old industrial packing pallet or two can be useful for raising cartons and baskets off of dirt or cement floors.

COLD STORAGE ORGANIZATION

TIP 471: *Watch out for odiferous vegetables*

Strong-smelling vegetables, such as cabbage and turnips, should be stored away from other vegetables that could absorb their odors. In fact, you may want to consider storing cabbages and turnips away from the house altogether, since their odors tend to linger for a long while. At the very least, keep odiferous vegetables away from celery, apples, and pears, which are particularly susceptible to absorbing strong odors. If space is tight, you can also wrap these foods in newspaper or hang in mesh bags away from other foods.

TIP 472: *Hang up your onions*

Onions are best stored off the ground and with plenty of air circulation. If you have intact mesh bags that were used to hold store-bought onions or potatoes, those will work. Some people drop onions into the legs of pantyhose, tie a knot, and drop in another onion, creating an amusing onion chain that can be hung from the ceiling or a door.

TIP 473: *Know that some vegetables don't mix well with others*

Care should be taken when storing certain vegetables because they release ethylene gas, a ripening agent that hastens the decomposition of other produce. Apples, peaches, plums, pears, muskmelons, and tomatoes produce high amounts of ethylene and should be stored near vents, if possible, or at least higher than other foods. Keep fruits that produce ethylene away from potatoes and carrots, as the ethylene will cause those to spoil rapidly.

TIP 474: Smaller baskets and piles are better than huge mounds

🍓 Keeping container sizes and piles on the small to medium size has two advantages over big mounds of produce. Smaller containers will allow more air to circulate around vegetables and fruits so that moisture doesn't become trapped and cause mold and other problems. Smaller containers also allow you to more thoroughly inspect your produce in storage for signs of rot, mold, or damage from pests.

TIP 475: Don't store canned goods in the root cellar

🍓 If your root cellar or cold storage area has the right amount of humidity for vegetable and fruit storage, then it's too humid to store canned preserves. The humidity will work on the metal lids and can rust and compromise seals.

TIP 476: Know how to read the signs of problems in cold storage

🍓 Regularly inspect vegetables and fruits placed in cold storage to identify problems before they spread. If vegetables sprout and grow, the temperature is too warm. If potatoes, beets, or other vegetables begin to shrink and shrivel, the air is too dry. If there are small black droppings on the floor, well sorry, but you have rodents. Remove any damaged or rotting produce to keep the problem from spreading. If you can't correct the temperature or humidity, it's time to fire up the stove and cook or give away the produce you can't eat.

COLD STORAGE PRODUCE

TIP 477: *Pick the best produce for cold storage*

● Once picked, produce doesn't improve over time, so vegetables intended for cold storage should be picked at the peak of maturity. They should be unblemished and, of course, disease-free. Extra care should be taken in harvesting food for long-term storage to avoid bruising and other damage that could promote spoilage while in storage.

TIP 478: *Leave stems on most vegetables*

● Leaving 1–2in (2.5–5cm) of the stem on most vegetables, including pumpkins and winter squash, helps to prevent water loss and increases the lifespan in storage. Notable exceptions are carrots and beets. Cut or snap off the green tops. If left on, the greens will deplete the vegetables of moisture and hasten deterioration.

TIP 479: Don't scrub—or even wash—most vegetables and fruits before storing

🍓 As important as washing and cleanliness are to most home food preservation projects, cold storage is the exception. Most produce stores better if it is not washed before storing since even if the produce is dried after washing, the added moisture is enough to encourage mold. Instead of washing, gently wipe or brush dirt and debris from produce and inspect carefully for pests that might be hitchhiking along.

TIP 480: Pick and store the best apples

🍓 In general, heirloom or antique apple varieties don't keep as well as some newer varieties, although there are some notable exceptions. Tart apples also are better keepers than sweet apples. Pick mature, unblemished apples and wrap them individually in newspaper. Keep wrapped apples in crates or cardboard boxes. Apples will keep for 2–7 months in cold storage, depending on the variety. Good storing varieties include Winter Banana, Fuji, Honey Crisp, and Newton Pippin, although there are other excellent varieties for cold storage.

TIP 481: *Some vegetables must be cured before storing*

● Some vegetables, such as potatoes, sweet potatoes, onions, and winter squashes, must be cured before storing to allow their skins to toughen enough for cold storage. Harvest these vegetables once they are fully mature or they will not store well. It is best to harvest on a dry day to avoid having moist soil caked on the produce. Onions and garlic should be exposed to the sun for curing. Cure other vegetables, such as potatoes, out of direct sun and the elements. The length of time will depend on the vegetable. Pumpkins and winter squash may need weeks before their skins are tough enough for storage.

TIP 482: *Don't use potatoes that have turned green*

● Potatoes are one of the favorite cold storage vegetables. If they are exposed to light, however, don't eat them. The green color is chlorophyll. By itself chlorophyll is not toxic, but it is a bit like the canary in the coal mine. It is an indicator that the potato has an increased production of solanine, which can cause illness or, in extreme cases (and large doses), death. Remove all green portions of the potato as well as the eyes, which are high in solanine. And, of course, keep potatoes away from light in the root cellar.

TIP 483: *Use your root cellar to grow fresh mushrooms*

● The root cellar is usually thought of as just a place for storage. But it can also be an excellent place to grow your own mushrooms. Kits are available that will provide you with everything you need—container, mushroom spores, growing medium. It's the perfect basement garden.

BEYOND THE BASICS

Once you've mastered the preserving fundamentals you may be inspired to host parties or enter your creations in your county fair competitions. More than one successful specialty foods entrepreneur started out as a home preserver! One of the joys of home preserving is passing along knowledge and tradition to others. Here are some tips for doing just that.

BRANCH OUT

TIP 484: *Find ways to improve your knowledge and your cooking*

● The more you know about food, the better cook you will be. If you are a good cook now, you can be a great cook by gaining some additional knowledge. This knowledge is not just a matter of trying different recipes, although that can be a part of it because, after all, practical experience is an excellent teacher. But knowing everything you can about culinary techniques, different types of foods you may never have heard of before, distinguishing between a good meal and one that is truly exceptional, understanding how to slow down and really taste the foods you are cooking so that you can create the best flavors possible—these are all knowledge and skills that can be learned.

You can learn quite a lot on your own by reading books, taking local classes, careful browsing of grocery stores and specialty food stores, and eating at ethnic restaurants. Magazines such as *Fine Cooking* and *Cook's Illustrated* have step-by-step articles on techniques. Many of these publications have branched out and are offering online instructional videos for free. The time you spend isn't wasted because it will all be stored on the shelves of the culinary library in your head and put to use in the kitchen.

TIP 485: *Pursue other foodie adventures*

⬤ Once you experience the satisfaction and power home food preserving gives you over your food supply, you could very well decide to branch out into other foodie pursuits. For example, you could explore the world of fermented breads. If you do, it would be great fun to have a backyard bread- or pizza-baking oven to cook those breads. If you are going to make ovenfired pizza, you will need to have some cheese to put on that pizza. You could make it! If you learn to make cheese, you will have a ready supply of whey for your whey fermenting projects. What is pizza without a glass of wine or bread without a cup of mead? If you decide to home brew wine, beer, cider, or mead, much of the same equipment you use for those activities can be used in fermenting. See how well this foodie logic works?

TIP 486: *Grow a home garden*

⬤ If you're not already a gardener when you begin preserving your own foods, you might be inspired to become one once you see all the possibilities that home preserving offers. Growing your own food ensures you know how your food was treated before it ever reaches your kitchen. You can be assured that your foods are organic—or at least that no harmful pesticides have been used during growing. You can have a steady supply of cucumbers and other vegetables without the waxes or paraffin routinely used by grocery stores to extend display life. You can grow thousands of varieties of vegetables you could never find in grocery stores or even in farmers' markets. You can monitor and harvest fruits, vegetables, and herbs at the very peak of ripeness.

TIP 487: *Grow microgreens for year-round salads*

⚫ One food type that just doesn't store well for more than a few days are salad greens. Although you can't store them, you can still have them if you grow your own microgreens. Microgreens are the baby seedlings of plants that are usually harvested when they are just a few days old. They are tender, nutritious, and can range from mild to spicy. You can toss them in salads, into entrées, or pile them on pizzas.

You can grow microgreens inside under grow lights or on a sunny windowsill. You don't need much more than a shallow pan, growing medium, and seeds. Microgreen varieties include cress, arugula, broccoli, cabbage, celery, clover, flax, chives, kale, mustard greens—the list goes on. Some companies sell microgreen mixes, but you can make your own with your favorite varieties.

TIP 488: *Barter and trade your preserves*

⚫ Parlay your skills at home preserving to stock your larder with foods you can't produce or get things done around the house. Perhaps you could partner with a vegetable gardener who can provide you with fresh produce in exchange for a share of canned goods. There are plenty of people who raise hens and have extra eggs they would be willing to swap for some canned tomatoes or a basket of berry jams. Or you could barter a half day of home canning and food drying for a half day of yard raking or other household chores.

Put the word out on Facebook community pages or other social media and see what types of mutually beneficial relationships you can strike up. Be very clear about deliverables and expectations. And if you're bargaining with someone you don't know, take all the usual and sensible precautions for dealing with strangers.

TIP 489: *Build and stock an emergency foods pantry*

If all the news stories about hurricanes, tornadoes, and earthquakes have you a little worried, you might be ready to embrace the idea of storing large quantities of food to get you and your family through a major natural disaster. Even if your attitude is a bit more laid back, it's a good idea to have at least a few days' supply of food and water in case there is a power outage that lasts a few days. You will have more food options by having a well-rounded supply of stored and preserved foods, including your root cellar supplies and dried foods.

Think through how your family eats and what types of foods you can put by to get through a few days without power or being able to open and close the refrigerator and freezer doors. Multi-functional foods, such as beans, tomatoes, and other canned vegetables can be combined with rice and pasta for a wide variety of chilies, soups, or stews that you can easily prepare on a camp stove or outdoor grill. Canned tuna and chicken can provide protein and satisfy the meat eaters in the crowd. Dried apples, canned peaches, and other treats can satisfy those in your survival party with a sweet tooth. High-energy snacks, such as trail mix and pumpkin and sunflower seeds are easy to store. Don't forget to have other basics too, such as bottled water, paper plates, and cups.

TIP 490: *Become a once-a-month cook*

⬤ Once-a-month cooking is just what it sounds like—preparing and storing away a month's worth of meals at one time, usually over a couple of days. There are many reasons there is a growing number of people interested in once-a-month cooking. Busy jobs and school schedules, a desire for a ready supply of home-cooked dinners and wanting to be as efficient as possible in the kitchen are common reasons. Some people are doing once-a-month cooking for frail or disabled family members who live in their own homes but who can't cook for themselves on a daily basis. Canning, freezing, and other food preservation methods go hand-in-hand with this cooking style.

There are whole websites and books devoted to providing tips on how to cook a month of meals at once, including how to plan meals, shop, multitask in the kitchen, and pack and store food. If once-a-month cooking sounds too ambitious, then try once-a-week and see how it works for you and your family.

SHARE THE FUN

TIP 491: *Involve your kids*

Kids learn by example. By involving your kids in your home preserving project, you'll be teaching them the importance of good, healthy foods and the ability to do things for themselves. Cooking together also reinforces skills, such as careful measuring and the ability to follow directions. To avoid frustration (for everyone!) or possible injury, think through a family preserving project together before inviting your kids into the kitchen. Make choosing the recipe a family discussion by checking books out of the library or perusing recipes together online. Discuss the importance of fresh produce and go to the store, farmers' market, or pick-your-own farm to get what you'll need.

Kids can be impatient with long and complex projects. Depending on their ages you may want to do some or all of the preparatory work without them and invite them into the kitchen when they will be interested in what you're doing. But save chores such as capping strawberries and snapping green beans for the kids to help. Of course, parts of the project that involve boiling water and hot jars should be left to the adults. This is a good time to talk about kitchen safety. Don't forget to get creative with names and labels for your creations.

TIP 492: *Give the gift of home preserved foods*

⬤ What better gifts than a jar of homemade figs in honey syrup or martini onions? Take particular care when labeling preserves you give to other people. Any food you preserve will need to be labeled with the name of the product and the date it was prepared. For gifts, it is helpful to include information about exactly how a product should be stored, when it should be considered expired, and serving suggestions. Include other handling information, such as how to defrost and cook. An ingredient list is also helpful, particularly for people who have food allergies.

TIP 493: *Create unique decorative labels for your foods*

⬤ Taking a few minutes to label your home preserves is important so that you know the contents and processing date. But labels don't have to be just functional; they can be attractive as well. And let's face it, if a food looks pretty, you—and the rest of your family—are more likely to eat it! Craft and art supply stores have art and scrapbooking materials that make beautiful labels. Add ribbons, fabric, or raffia that can also serve to hold hang tags. You can also order custom labels online or download and print pre-designed labels. Of course, if you're very handy with graphic design software, the sky's the limit.

TIP 494: *Make jam with your friends*

Hosting a home canning party is a fun way to share the satisfaction and fun of your home canning interests. To ensure your party is a success, think through logistics carefully and communicate requirements and expectations to guests ahead of time so there are no surprises. Only invite as many people as can fit comfortably in your kitchen. (It might be a small party!) Ask guests to wear their own fun or fancy aprons as party attire. Offer snacks to keep everyone fueled up and energized during the canning project.

Select a single recipe that appeals to everyone, such as strawberry or blueberry jam. Survey guests to find out how many jars of jam they would like to take home after the party. Have guests bring their own jars and lids or ask guests to pitch money into the pot to buy supplies and produce. You could even coordinate your canning party with a trip to a pick-your-own farm or outing to a local farmers' market.

Take an inventory of the equipment you'll need and ask guests to bring what you don't already have in your own kitchen. Make a checklist for your canning project outlining the workflow and post it the day of the party so all the guests can see what is involved and what jobs need to be done. Jobs may include preparing produce, stirring jam, tending the hot-water bath canner, creating decorative labels, and cleaning up.

Depending on the number of party guests, you will probably make two, three, or even more batches of jam, so get hot water boiling while guests get to work washing and preparing produce. Remember to block out plenty of time. Many hands make for fast work, but chatting and getting everyone coordinated might take more time than you expect.

At the end of the party, have small bags or baskets ready for guests to load up their jam. You can even tuck in a recipe card as a souvenir.

TIP 495: *Find friends who share your interest in home food preserving*

⬤ Depending on where you live, it may be difficult to find friends who share your interest in home food preserving. If you want to share tips, recipes, and perhaps even equipment with people who live close to you, you can begin by looking into groups sponsored by your local public library or county agricultural extension services. If there are no dedicated food preserving groups, then groups devoted to local foods, simple living, gardening, and cooking are good places to start since people there will likely have some interest in food preserving.

You can also find new friends in far-flung places by using social media on the Internet. Visit and comment on blogs about home food preserving—or start your own. Like and comment on Facebook pages dedicated to canning, freezing, or other home food preserving methods. There are thousands of bulletin board discussions with active and involved members who will welcome a stranger with similar interests. Over time, friendships develop through information and recipe swapping and can turn from virtual to real-life friends.

TIP 496: *Organize a preserve swap*

⬤ Trading your preserves with others is a fun and easy way to increase the variety of the foods in your pantry without putting in a lot of extra work. Many people put up far more jars of chow chow than their family can eat and others put up too many jars of applesauce. Share all that bounty! Alert other food preservers you know that you plan to organize a food swap after the height of canning season—usually in the fall. Preservers can sign up on a wish list for foods they hope to get from others in an exchange. It's best not to have everyone make delivery promises since the vagaries of life and the unpredictability of harvests can always interfere with the best of intentions.

BECOME A PRO

TIP 497: *Become a Master Food Preserver*

 Many people have heard of the Master Gardener program. But did you know that some counties and states also have a Master Food Preserver program? Like the Master Gardener program, Master Food Preserver programs provides volunteers with extensive skills education and certification in exchange for volunteer help in such jobs as answering telephones, judging county and state fair competitions, and helping in community canning kitchens. To find out if your county participates in the Master Food Preserver program, contact your county agricultural extension agent.

TIP 498: *Develop your own recipes*

Once you have some experience and a successful track record, you may want to try your hand at developing your own recipes. There are well-researched USDA guidelines for safe preserving that you should know and follow for safe preserving. If you are serious about recipe development and even considering selling your canned goods, you may want to invest in a pH meter, sold by science supply companies, or even send samples to a third-party lab for pH testing.

TIP 499: *Enter the world of competitive canning*

● If your homemade preserves are winning compliments from friends and family, you may want to see how your efforts compare with other home preservers. County and state fairs competitions have extensive categories for home preserves. Make sure you study the fair's competitive handbook for rules and entry requirements, which specify everything from jar type to how the preserve is filled and processed. Failing to follow even one of the strict details can disqualify you from competition or cause you to lose valuable points. You probably won't get rich by winning competitive canning awards. But competing offers other rewards. Certainly you will learn a great deal about what is considered a quality canned product. It is also a great way to meet people who share your interest in preserving foods.

TIP 500: *Start a specialty foods business*

● You have a recipe and a product everyone is asking for. Maybe it's time to start your own food products business. You will need to investigate zoning laws, set up a licensed kitchen, procure liability insurance and follow food preparation, testing, and labeling regulations. There are a host of other requirements spelled out in local, state, and federal regulations. You may need the help of a lawyer to navigate the maze of getting a food to market.

Talk with other food entrepreneurs about their experiences. Some of them have written informative and useful books. Search online for discussion groups of people in the business. Contact your local chamber of commerce to inquire about mentoring programs. And look into state resources for small business loans and even incubator programs designed to help small businesses get started. If the process of producing the food yourself is out of the question, research co-packers—companies that will use (and perhaps improve) your recipes, produce, and pack the product for you.

THE HOME PRESERVER'S KITCHEN

Not all of the items listed here are necessary to get started with your first home preserving project. But these items do represent a fairly complete home preserving kitchen and can serve as a checklist when out shopping or garage sale hopping.

GENERAL KITCHEN EQUIPMENT
• 8-quart pot
• 4-quart pot
• 2- or 3-quart saucepan
• Double boiler
• Kitchen timer
• Wooden or plastic long-handled spoons
• Slotted spoon
• Spatula
• Potato masher or meat pounder
• Tongs
• Funnels
• Kitchen shears
• Mixing bowls
• Cutting boards
• Various knives
• Vegetable brush
• Large trays
• Kitchen scale
• Food mill, blender, or food processor
• Mandoline slicer

• Colander
• Sieve
• Kitchen scale
• Measuring cups and spoons
• Instant read thermometer
• Towels, washcloths
• Bottle cleaning brushes
• Cheesecloth
• Paper towels
• Apron
• Rubber or latex gloves
• Pot holders
• Hot pads
• Labels
• Waterproof pen
• Kitchen notebook

Specialized Produce Preparation Supplies
• Vegetable peeler
• Zester
• Apple corer
• Cherry pitter
• Melon baller
• Strawberry capper
• Pear corer
• Pitting spoon
• Vegetable or potato masher

Canning
- Specialized jam pot
- Hot-water bath canner, with rack
- Pressure canner, with rack
- Jars and lids
- Jar lifter
- Lid lifter
- Bubble remover
- Foam skimmer
- Ladle
- Wide-mouth funnel
- Cheesecloth or jelly bag
- Candy thermometer

Freezing
- Food-grade plastic freezer containers
- Food-grade plastic freezer bags and paper
- Heavy-duty aluminum foil
- Vacuum sealer and bags
- Freezer thermometer

Drying
- Dehydrator, solar dryer, or oven
- Needle and dental floss
- Vacuum sealer and bags
- Glass jars and lids
- Food-grade plastic containers and lids

Fermenting
- Stoneware or glass fermentation crock with weight
- Fermentation containers with air locks (buckets, bottles, jars, and crocks)
- Food-grade plastic buckets or beverage fermenting containers
- Food-grade plastic storage containers with lids
- Glass jars and lids
- Glass vinegar or wine bottles and stoppers

Salting and Curing
- Smoker
- Meat thermometer
- Butchering knives
- Deboning knife
- Knife sharpener
- Meat grinder (for sausage making)
- Brine pump
- Stoneware or glass fermentation crock with weight
- Wide-mouth canning jars
- Enamelware canner
- Moisture-proof wrapping
- Stockinette for holding meat wrap after packaging
- Muslin

Cold Storage/Root Cellar
- Packing supplies
- Baskets and crates
- Shelving

HOT-WATER BATH CANNER HIGH-ALTITUDE ADJUSTMENTS

Elevation	Time to Add to Processing Time
1,001 to 3,000ft	5 minutes
3,001 to 6,000ft	10 minutes
6,001 to 8,000ft	15 minutes
8,001 to 10,000ft	20 minutes

PRESSURE CANNER HIGH-ALTITUDE ADJUSTMENTS

Altitude	Dial-Gauge Pressure Canner	Weighted-Gauge Pressure Canner
1 to 1,000ft	11lb	10lb
1,001 to 2,000ft	11lb	15lb
2,001 to 4,000ft	12lb	15lb
4,001 to 6,000ft	13lb	15lb
6,001 to 8,000ft	14lb	15lb
8,001 to 10,000ft	15lb	15lb

INDEX